FIELD ARCHERY
AND
BOWHUNTING

ARNOLD O. HAUGEN

Iowa State University

and

HARLAN G. METCALF

State University of New York
College at Cortland

THE RONALD PRESS COMPANY • NEW YORK

Library of Congress Catalog Card Number: 63–22597

PRINTED IN THE UNITED STATES OF AMERICA

Dedicated
to
our wives
Vneda Haugen
and
Margaret Metcalf
whose constructive criticism, constant understanding, inspiration, and encouragement made our
efforts possible.

Preface

This book on techniques for field and hunting archery will satisfy a long-felt need. The individual archer interested in improving his shooting, or learning to shoot good bare-bow field archery, will find an organized approach to teaching himself the ancient art of instinctive bow shooting. The archer instructor in school, camp, and recreational programs will find here for the first time a complete outline of lessons on how to teach bare-bow field archery.

Experienced bowhunters may find here some new hunting lore to test. Beginning bowhunters will find guidelines to help them develop proficiency for successful hunting.

Archery is a sport for all ages. It offers a lifetime challenge. This book brings together the experiences of the authors who have enjoyed and promoted archery for many years. Their activities have covered every phase of archery, including bowmaking; teaching archery in colleges, schools, and camps; and administration of archery in recreation programs.

The authors wish to acknowledge the generous help of many individuals who assisted in some way to make this book possible. Among these are Audrey Hein and Elsa Gray of the National Field Archery Association; Dr. C. N. Hickman of Jackson Heights, New York; Forrest Huntley, Eugene, Oregon; Ed and Myrtle Miller of Upper Saddle River, New Jersey, directors of the Teela-Wooket Archery Training Camp; Dr. Jay B. Nash of New York City; Earl Ullrich, Roseburg, Oregon; Bert Wallis, Sequim, Washington; Dick Wilson, Kalamazoo, Michigan; Dr. Lyle Sowls, Tucson, Arizona; and John and Vera Yount, Redlands, California.

Special thanks are due the Michigan Conservation and Alabama Conservation magazines for permission to reuse materials previously published in those organs. For the use of certain photographs, thanks are due Auburn University, Iowa State University, the Michigan Conservation Department, and the Tennessee Conservation Department. Individuals who kindly provided photos include David J. Crowley, Jr., Dedham, Massachusetts; Mrs. Frances Emmerling, Avon Lake, Ohio; Dr. D. A. Hindman, Columbia,

Missouri; W. Leon Riegler, Kalamazoo, Michigan; and Frank Spaulding, Cortland, New York. Permission to use various cartoon figures by Oscar Warbach of Lansing, Michigan, is greatly appreciated. Except where otherwise indicated, photographs are by author A. O. Haugen.

ARNOLD O. HAUGEN
HARLAN G. METCALF

Ames, Iowa
Cortland, New York
October, 1963

Contents

viii Contents

I

FIELD ARCHERY

1

Field Archery Equipment

A field archer to be properly equipped needs a bow of proper weight for his strength, a set of matched arrows, an armguard, fingertabs or a shooting glove, and a quiver (Fig. 1–1). Physical strength, experience of the shooter, sex, age, and the type of round to be shot, all influence the final choice of equipment.

BOWS

The beginning field archer today is fortunate in that he has a wide latitude of choice in bows. When buying his first bow, he will be wise to avoid the cheapest wood bows, such as lemonwood and hickory, and to secure one of glass construction. His selection will most likely be between a moulded all fiberglass bow and a laminated bow made from layers of wood and fiberglass. A bow of the latter type will vary in price depending on whether it is of the straight-limbed or the working-recurve type (see Fig. 5–1).

A young man in his late teens and of average strength will do well to purchase the bow of his choice with a pull that does not exceed 35 lbs. at 28 inches of draw. Weights stamped on men's bows usually are determined at this length of draw. An individual of less than average strength will do well to select a bow 5 lbs. lighter, whereas a muscular person may wish to select one 5 lbs. heavier.

Any person who has the good fortune to learn to shoot with school, camp, or borrowed equipment is in the enviable position of being able to make his first purchased bow one of better quality and of the appropriate weight to fit his future field archery needs. A trained field archer usually does his competitive shooting with a bow that has a pull of between 40 and 45 lbs. at his length of draw.

College-age women on an average do best if they learn to shoot with bows that have a pull of about 20 lbs. at 26 inches of draw. Weaker or stronger women should use bows 2 or 3 lbs. lighter or stronger, depending on their physical ability. Once properly trained in techniques, the average woman field archer usually does her best shooting with a bow that has a pull of between 25 and 30 lbs. at the length of arrow she draws.

Bows recommended for college-class instruction are usually suitable for any beginning archer. Light bows are recommended so that the archer can

3

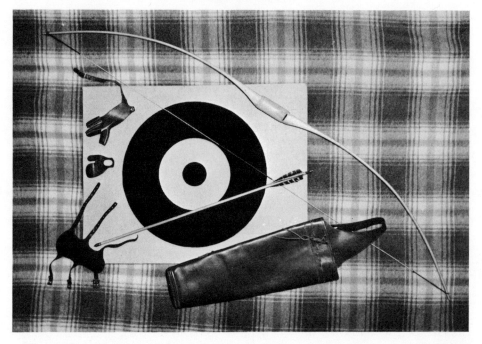

Fig. 1–1. Equipment of the beginning field archer may consist of a set of arrows, an armguard, a fingertab (or shooting glove), a straight-limbed bow, and a shoulder quiver.

concentrate on learning the proper techniques. Such equipment has adequate cast for the short distances at which a beginning archer should train. He should practice until he can consistently hit a 6-inch target at close distances before moving back to distances exceeding 20 yards. This is a matter of common sense. Why shoot at a distance at which you cannot hit your target with some consistency?

Any man or woman seriously considering tournament shooting should invest in a glass and wood laminated working-recurve bow. In purchasing such high-quality bows, it is recommended that the archer make his purchase from an establishment that has an experienced archer in its sales department. It is important to be on guard against being pressured into buying a bow that is stronger than you can handle without straining. A man's bow above 50 lbs. is considered unnecessarily heavy as far as field archery is concerned.

ARROWS

Port Orford cedar arrows are the usual type used by beginning archers. Such arrows can vary from very poor to very good. The cheaper ones are inferior in that they are not matched for spine or weight, with the result that no two arrows shoot alike, even if the technique of the archer is faultless.

The more moderately priced arrows are matched for spine so that they will shoot with less lateral dispersal. This arrow is of adequate quality for physical education classes and for beginning individuals.

As soon as a student has learned the technique of field archery and has shot enough to know the proper length of his draw, it is recommended that he buy a set of good-quality arrows for himself. He has a choice between wood, glass, or aluminum arrows, depending on the quality desired and on how much he wishes to spend. If he chooses to purchase Port Orford cedar shafts, he ought to look for a set that is matched for both spine and weight. In general, however, he will be wiser to invest in a set of good-quality hollow glass shafted arrows so that he can do his very best at hitting the mark. Glass arrows are almost unbreakable; they remain straight and are unaffected by heat or moisture. Over a period of time, their durability will save their owner money.

Glass shafts of 5/16-inch diameter shoot well in quality bows with a pull of from 25 to 30 lbs. Bows 35 to 40 lbs. in weight generally require the 21/64-inch diameter arrows, and bows of more than 40 lbs. usually require the 11/32-inch size arrows.

Target points on the arrows are preferred if the shooting is done at close quarters at regulation target bosses. When purchasing your shafts, be certain that they are matched to the weight of your bow. If you purchase wooden arrows, make certain that the shafts are straight. Wooden arrows that have been in a show window where the sun has "baked" them are probably crooked. The price is the same, straight or crooked, so insist on straight ones.

Proper length of arrows used is of prime importance. An arrow that is too short is dangerous to shoot because, if it is overdrawn, the point might pierce the archer's hand, or it might lodge against the back of the bow so that on release it might break or ram splinters into the arm or hand of the shooter. Any arrow that is too long usually results in uneven lengths of draw from shot to shot because the length of draw cannot be checked readily. For information on how to determine proper length of arrow see Fig. A–4.

ARMGUARDS

An armguard is necessary to properly protect the inside of the forearm and wrist area from painful slaps by the bowstring. It has a secondary function in keeping loose clothing such as a sleeve out of the way of the string so as to give the string a clear path along which to travel in projecting the shaft toward the target. Clothing, if it interferes with the string, causes the arrow to be deflected off course and to drop low. Experiments by researchers have shown that a bowstring on proper release actually does not hit the armguard on the way forward, but gives it a slap as it vibrates backwards again.

SHOOTING GLOVES OR FINGERTABS

Protection for the fingers that draw the bowstring is essential for two reasons. First, it keeps the fingers from getting blistered and sore from pressure and scraping of the string; and second, it provides a smooth and slippery surface for the string to slide off of at the release. Some archers prefer fingertabs (see Fig. 1–1). They are reasonable in cost, give the archer a good "feel" of the string, and provide the smoothest release, especially with a light bow. When using fingertabs, the archer may find it to his advantage to trim off some of the length from the front edge so as to eliminate the floppy tip that overhangs the index finger and interferes with the "feel" of that finger at the corner of the mouth at full-draw anchor.

Shooting gloves are normally used with bows that are of such a heavy pull that they result in sore fingers if a light tab is used. Sometimes referred to as fingerstalls, these gloves consist of three fingerstalls that completely cover and protect the three string fingers up to the second joint. Many of the best archers in the nation use shooting gloves. When they are used, there is almost no chance for sore fingers, even with bows with 60 or more pounds of pull.

To provide the best possible release, some archers rub the surface of their tabs or glove with paraffin. Others dust talcum powder on the working surface of the tabs and gloves to help facilitate a smooth release.

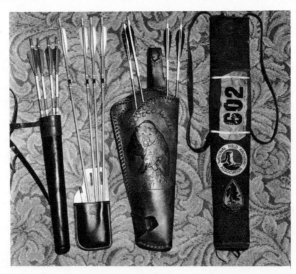

Fig. 1–2. Quivers used for field archery consist of four general types. At the far left is a type commonly used in women's physical education classes. It is suspended from a belt around the waist. The second is a man's hip pocket quiver, the third is a shoulder quiver commonly used for field shooting and bow-hunting, and the fourth is a middle-of-the-back quiver sometimes used for field archery but more commonly used for hunting.

QUIVERS

A variety of quivers is available for archers (Fig. 1–2). The cheapest, a type that can be used only by men, is the hip pocket quiver. Belt-type target quivers are most suitable for women's physical education classes and target competition. The type with a belt hook is most convenient. The shoulder-type quiver is most commonly used in competitive shooting.

Archery is like many other sports in that one can invest a little or a lot and have much fun and recreation at either level of investment. Equipment good enough to enter competitive events in other field sports such as rifle or skeet matches or golf requires a larger investment than is needed for archery. Archery, accordingly, is an economical sport; but it does not come free of cost. Its many attributes make it worth every dollar invested. How many other sports can be participated in from youth to old age and be enjoyed as family-type recreation?

2

Learning To Shoot Field Style

INTRODUCTION

Nothing takes the place of practice for developing and maintaining proficiency in archery. Good results, however, depend on practicing with sound techniques. The purpose of this chapter is to present, in an orderly sequence, sound basic techniques for learning field and hunting-style archery shooting. These techniques, if followed carefully and faithfully, will enable an archer, in a few weeks' time, to improve his shooting. With the resultant gain in skill, the archer will have enhanced both his ability to hit the mark and his chances for success in hunting. Such results will provide greater enjoyment from participation in the age-old sport of archery.

TYPES OF ARCHERY

Roughly speaking, archery today can be grouped into two major types: field and target archery. In *field archery,* the official competitive rounds consist of two 14-target units, each with the targets at distances usually varying from 20 feet to 80 yards. The faces usually have two scoring rings. In *target archery,* however, specified numbers of arrows are shot in rounds with known target distances and at faces with either five or ten scoring rings.

Field archery as defined by the *Official Handbook of Field Archery* is the use of the bow and arrow in the shooting at animated and inanimated objects. Until recently it consisted of unknown, unannounced, and not predetermined distances. This definition includes conditions inherent in hunting legal game of all kinds, and in various field games (described in Chapter 3). Practice under such conditions develops the archer's accuracy in shooting and his skill in judging distances. Such abilities in turn improve his chances for success in "bringing home the bacon" when hunting.

The most popular and universally used field game is the official Field Round of the National Field Archery Association. This round consists of 28 targets, made up of two units of 14 targets each, or twice around one 14-target unit, arranged to simulate realistic hunting situations for big and small game. Varied terrain with different conditions of light and shadow at unknown distances increases the interest of the round.

The National Field Archery Association was the result of organizational efforts of archers primarily interested in hunting and informal roving. The shooting style used by most of these archers was called "instinctive" since it was assumed to be a natural innate coordination—as natural as shooting marbles or throwing stones. In this style no artificial sighting device such as a "point of aim" or "bowsight" was used. The field or roving archer drew the arrow back to a high "side-of-the-face" anchor (closer to the eye than the usual under-the-chin target anchor), kept both eyes open, stared intently at the smallest spot within the center of the object to be hit, and released the arrow.

This "field" style of shooting, long referred to as instinctive, is also called the "bare-bow" style. The bow is bare, or barren of any sighting device. "Instinctive," "bare-bow," and "field" styles all are synonymous terms; but this book will use the term "bare-bow" style.

A few years after the founding of the N.F.A.A. and after many state and local field archery associations and clubs had formed, another type of archer appeared in increasing numbers on the field courses. He was the sight shooter commonly referred to as a "free-style" archer. A separate class of competition called the "Free-Style Division" eventually was provided for these newcomers. Actually, the term "free-style" is a misnomer. It would have been far more descriptive to have named this group the "Sight Division." Since sight shooting in reality is a form of target archery, there is little need to cover that phase of shooting here.

PRINCIPLES OF SHOOTING THE BOW AND ARROW

In learning to shoot a bow, there are certain fundamenal principles involved. These principles are as important today as when they were first discussed by Roger Ascham (1544) of England. The only difference is that today seven fundamentals for good technique are recognized, whereas in Ascham's time six were considered.

The seven fundamental principles of archery shooting and their component parts will first be listed, then followed with a discussion on how they are executed in bare-bow (instinctive) shooting.

1. *The Stance*
    a) Relation of body and face to the target
    b) Body alignment and distribution of weight
2. *Nocking the Arrow*
    a) Cock and hen feathers
    b) Placement of arrow on the string
3. *The Draw*
    a) Positions of left shoulder, elbow, wrist, and fingers
    b) Positions of right shoulder, elbow, forearm, wrist, and fingers

4. *Anchor*
   a) Position of string or arrow hand on right side of face and jaw
5. *Aim*
   a) "Aiming"
   b) Holding
6. *Release*
   a) Secondary draw
   b) Use of muscles that bring the shoulder blade and elbow back
7. *Afterhold or Follow-Through*
   a) Position of bow arm and hand
   b) Position of drawing arm and hand

Every one of these seven fundamentals and their parts must be executed the same way each time in order for the arrows to fly consistently straight. Furthermore, each fundamental must be executed in its proper and logical sequence.

With diligent practice an archer will develop the habit of automatically executing each fundamental correctly and in proper sequence. An important point in shooting a bow is to be able to diagnose the cause of trouble if and when trouble develops with one's shooting. For example, suppose arrows for some unknown reason consistently go to the left and there is no friend to observe and report faulty technique. How then does the archer figure out what is wrong? At such a time, if the archer will concentrate on properly executing each fundamental in sequence, he will usually discover and "iron out" his own fault. In this case, with the arrows going to the left, he reviews carefully, first his stance, then the nocking of his arrow, and then the draw. While checking details of his draw, he may discover that in his anxiety about faulty shooting he has become tense and is gripping his bow handle tightly, generally considered a fault. He relaxes his grip and the arrows now go straight. A good archer usually is adept at diagnosing the fault, or faults, contributing to his missing the target.

Each of the seven fundamentals of archery will now be discussed in detail and in proper sequence.

1. THE STANCE. For the right-handed archer, the left side of the body will be toward the target, and the front of the body faces 90 degrees to the right. The head and face must be turned left toward the target, looking over the left shoulder.

Most archers take a stance with the feet spread about as far apart as the width of their hips. This provides a comfortable and well-balanced stance with the weight equally distributed on both feet. If this stance does not feel right, adjust the spread slightly until it feels comfortable. The feet should be parallel to each other and at right angles to the line to the target (Fig. 2–1).

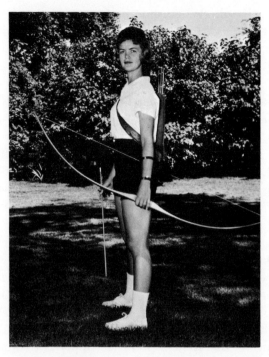

Fig. 2–1. Miss Sonja Haugen demonstrates the beauty, balance, and poise of the correct *stance*—fundamental No. 1 for archers.

The body should be erect, with the torso, hips, and legs well aligned. The top of the head should be tipped a couple of inches diagonally forward and toward the right. This will in a way fit the archer's head to the bow, which should be canted (upper limb tipped) to the right about 20 degrees in order that the archer may see his target or game with both eyes at once. This allows making full use of man's bifocal vision, which is useful in perceiving distance. Other variations in the stance of the field archer might involve spreading the feet farther apart to add stability on uneven ground, a crouched position to permit aiming underneath overhanging branches, or kneeling on one knee to keep partially hidden while shooting at game. Field and hunting archers, although usually more adept at shooting from an erect stance, while hunting at least, must have the ability to shoot from whatever position they may be in when game is sighted.

2. NOCKING THE ARROW. For the right-handed archer, the arrow must be placed on the left side of the bow; and if it is a three-feathered arrow, it must be so nocked on the string that the cock feather (the one perpendicular to the bowstring when nocked) always faces outward, directly away from the bow. In this position, the other two feathers (hen feathers) will bypass the bow smoothly and the cockfeather (usually the odd-colored one) will not be injured. When shooting arrows fletched with four vanes, this precaution is unnecessary.

Modern hunting arrows are usually equipped with index nocks to indicate which is the cock feather. Such nocks have a ridge or rise on the side of the nock corresponding to the cock feather. This is so that any hunter who uses arrows with three feathers can determine which is the cock feather and to nock his arrow without looking away from his game.

It is important that the archer place the nocks of his arrows at the exact same spot on the serving of the string for every shot. Traditionally, to find this spot the archer places the arrow on the arrow-rest and places the nock end on the string at a point perpendicular to it. This place on the string is called the *nocking point*. In recent years, however, many archers have found it advantageous to move their nocking points 1/8 to 3/16 inches higher than this point (perpendicular to the string from the top of the arrow-rest). It is important that the nocking point on the string be clearly indicated so that each arrow can be nocked precisely at the exact same place. To accomplish such consistency, the archer should wind a 1/8-inch knot or lump of thread on the string (laid in quick-drying glue so that it will not slip up out of place) exactly adjacent to and touching the upper edge of the nocking point. Some archers prefer to apply two lumps of thread to the string, one above and one below the nocking point. Commercial nocking points are available, which can be laid on the serving of the string at the proper place and bound tightly in place with thread and glue. These may be satisfactory if they fit the end of the nock exactly, and if attached tightly enough to prevent their slipping out of place (see Fig. 2–2 and Fig. A–2).

3. THE DRAW. The principles and techniques involved in executing the draw properly are similar for all types of archery. Starting with the bow arm (or left arm for right-handed archers), the points to watch follow:

The *left shoulder* should be kept *down* and *back* in its natural position, the same height level as the right shoulder. If the archer persists in raising (hunching) the left shoulder and allowing it to come forward on the draw, it is a sign that he is "overbowed"—trying to use a bow that is too heavy for him to pull back to a full draw without straining. Another characteristic of an "overbowed" archer can readily be observed by watching the alignment of his back while he is shooting. Instead of the proper erect stance, his upper trunk usually leans away from the target, with the hips swayed toward the target.

The *left elbow* should point outward to the left so that if it were to bend, the forearm would swing inward toward the center of the chest. During the draw, the left elbow may be very slightly bent, if that is the only way the string will have clearance from hitting the inside middle of the arm section. If one can keep the left elbow locked straight while releasing the

Fig. 2–2. Miss Haugen demonstrates fundamental No. 2, *nocking* the arrow on the string. Note that the arrow is nocked perpendicular (or about ⅛ inch higher) to the string from where it lies on the arrow-rest just about the handle.

string, and finds that the string does not strike the inner side of the arm at the elbow, so much the better. You have one less thing to worry about. However, most women and some men when asked to straighten the left arm in a locked position will find the elbow joint bowed inward (toward the bowstring) in a position called hyperextension. If the arm is held in this position when the string is released, the string will hit this inner side of the arm inflicting a painful blow, resulting in a sore black-and-blue area that will remain for several days. An unfortunate experience like this discourages beginners from continuing in the sport of archery.

To prevent such a painful injury to the elbow area, some beginners move the leather armguard up the arm from its proper place at the wrist. It is much better, however, to remove the cause of the trouble by changing the position of the elbow. Whenever the string strikes the inner edge of the arm; the sleeve on a blouse, shirt, or jacket; or a pin on the left side of the chest, the speed of the string and the arrow will be slowed. Such an arrow will fall short and to the left of where it was aimed. The remedy to the problem is to roll the elbow out and upward and hold it in a position of very slight flexion, bent just enough so that the string clears the inner edge of the arm. Do not flex the elbow too much, for if you do it will cause the left arm to shake or quiver since too much strain will be put on the muscles that extend the elbow of the bow arm.

Another important precaution to prevent injury, especially to women archers, is to be sure always to draw the string into the region of the armpit and against the side of the torso or chest, never in front of or across the chest.

It is quite proper for the string to strike the inside of the left wrist a glancing blow, and it generally does. That is why it is imperative that one wear an armguard bracer of heavy leather to protect the wrist. This slap of the string against the armguard does not negatively influence the flight of the arrow on a properly executed shot since the slap actually occurs on the rebound of the string after the arrow has left.

The left wrist should be so relaxed that the tension of the bow against the left hand when the bow is being drawn will force the hand and wrist to flex back and up (a position of complete abduction). There are a considerable number of very good archers who do not use this abducted wrist and hand position on the bow handle. They strive instead to keep the back of the wrist straight and in line with the forearm and the back of the hand. This straight or extended-wrist position, however, is only proper when using a bow with a "pistol grip" type of handle. Such specially designed handles are becoming increasingly popular. The handles of such bows are formed to fit the hand so that the wrist can be held straight without undue strain. The archer does not have to use adductor muscles of the wrist to hold it straight.

Most beginning archers shoot bows with regular handles (not "pistol grip"), and they should relax their left wrists and allow the bow to force the wrist and hand into abduction. The wrist should be so relaxed in this position that when the string is released, the wrist and bow with it will spring forward into adduction from the recoil.

During the draw, and until the arrow has been released, the inside of the bow handle should rest against the thumb part of the palm of the hand. The upper part of the hand's contact with the bow handle is between the base of the thumb and the base of the index finger; the middle contact is against the inside of the fleshy pad below the base of the thumb. The lower contact of the hand with the bow handle should be at the middle of the heel of the hand (where it joins the middle of the wrist).

The left hand should not grip the bow handle but should be relaxed. With left hand and upper arm pushing against the bow, and the fingers of the right hand and shoulder drawing the string, it amounts to *separating* the bow and nocking point on the bowstring. In order to control the bow, the left index finger encircles the bow handle together with the left thumb, which should rest on top of or near the end of the index finger. Since controlling the bow so that it does not drop or bounce from the hand is more important in hunting archery than in competitive archery, it is permissible

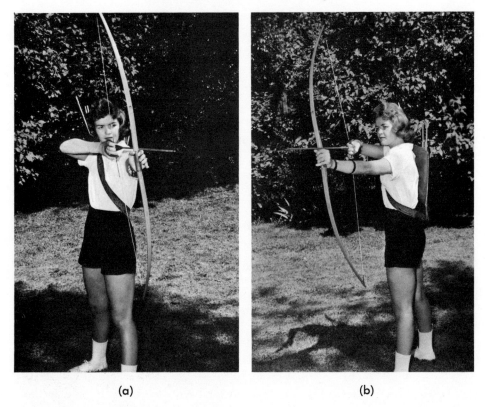

(a)   (b)

Fig. 2–3. Miss Haugen demonstrates two views of the *pre-draw aiming* position for the pre-draw gap system. In (a) note the right shoulder forward to
allow the fingers to contact the string, the canted bow, and the relaxed contact
of the bow hand on the bow. In both (a) and (b) note the slight tilt of the head
parallel to the canted bow so that when the string is brought back to anchor,
it will fit snugly against the side of the face without further motion or adjustment of the head. Note also that arrow, fingers, wrist, and elbow are all in the
same plane, and that the major features of balance and poise found in Fig. 2–1
are retained.

to allow the other fingers also to contact the bow handle, provided one is not
therefrom tempted to grip the bow (Figs. 2–3a and b).

The position of the right shoulder in all forms of archery is approximately at the same level as that of the left shoulder. In hunting or roving,
however, when shooting at something on the ground at less than 10 yards
distance, one must bend the body to the left toward the shot, which naturally brings the right shoulder higher than the left but in alignment toward
the target.

In most cases the right elbow should be slightly above shoulder height
where its position will be in a straight line with the tip and the nock of the
arrow. Some very good archers, however, shoot with their right elbow an

inch or so higher than this straight-line position. These archers get by with this variation from correct form by virtue of the fact that they generally have unusually long ring (third) fingers. If these archers had a shorter ring finger on the right hand, their fingers would tend to lose effective contact with the string whenever the elbow was too high. Such a condition commonly is known as "lazy third finger."

The Mediterranean release (draw) using the three middle fingers of the right hand (if right-handed) for pulling the string is used by practically all archers today. These three fingers are hooked over the string with the index finger above and the other two below the arrow. Care should be taken to establish the habit of placing these fingers so that they are perpendicular to the string. Grasp the string *in the outermost crease* of the fingers. Then as the draw is made, the string should roll slightly out of the crease and come to rest just behind the "fatpads" on the fingertips. It is difficult to relax the fingers and wrist if the string is grasped at a point any farther out on the finger to begin with. It is essential to have the fingers, wrist, and forearm relaxed or it will be impossible to keep them in the straight line with the arrow and elbow as previously mentioned.

4. ANCHOR. Each one of a box of rifle cartridges has the same measured and weighed amount of powder, and each of the lead bullets weighs the same. This makes for consistency in shooting. The rifleman can expect the same velocity, accuracy, and distance from each shell. The archer's anchor is one of the most important factors in helping him put the same amount of power ("powder") back of each arrow he shoots. It is a major key to accurate shooting.

Consistency depends on a definite precise anchor on the jaw and side of the face for each arrow aimed and shot. The other six of the seven fundamentals of archery techniques and their parts also are essential ingredients in the "load" for uniform power and for accurate delivery of the arrow.

For the *most commonly used field anchor,* make a U-shape arrangement with the thumb and index finger of the right hand. Place the fleshy base of this U behind the angle of the right jawbone with the thumb fitting snugly under the bone and against the neck. In this position the point of the thumb will be near your "Adam's apple," and the first joint (counting from the end of the thumb) will contact the under side of the angle of the jaw opposite the position of your tonsil. The top of the index finger should fit into the hollow underneath the cheekbone, touching it snugly with the second joint (from the end) just in front of as well as below the cheekbone. With this anchor the bow usually is canted (upper limb tipped) about 20 degrees to the right. The head should also be tipped correspondingly to the right (with the chin pulled in) in which position the right eye will be directly above the nock end of the arrow. The arrangement described

Fig. 2–4. Miss Haugen demonstrates the *field anchor* used in bare-bow shooting. Note the snug, firm side of face anchor, both eyes open and concentrating on the smallest spot in the center of the target, beautiful alignment of forearm with the arrow, and the relaxed grip on the bow handle.

literally fits the hand to the face and will permit a snug unified anchor (Figs. 2–4, 2–5, 2–6, and 2–7).

A modification of this field anchor that is sometimes used with success consists of placing the base of the thumb (second joint from end) snugly into the small depression directly under the right ear and behind the angle of the jawbone. The first joint of the index finger can rest on the cheekbone and curve around it if the head is in the normal position or tilted slightly forward. If the head is raised and tilted back a little, the index finger may lie underneath the cheekbone as in the more commonly used field anchor. In the modified variation, the hand is anchored farther out to the side of the face than usual. To compensate for this and to prevent the arrow going to the left, the bow and the archer's head both must be canted farther to the right, perhaps as much as 25 to 30 degrees, in order to bring the right eye directly above the nock, thereby permitting aiming directly at the target (Fig. 2–8).

(a)

(b)

(c)

Fig. 2–5. Miss Haugen demonstrates the *anchor* for field shooting as seen from three different views. From above (a), from below and behind the jaw (b), and from the rear (c). Note the alignment of the elbow and forearm with the arrow.

Fig. 2-6. Dr. Arnold Haugen demonstrates the field *anchor* most commonly used by bare-bow field archers at the Teela-Wooket Archery Camp. (Photograph by D. Crowley, Jr.)

Fig. 2-7. Stuart Thomas, a student at the Teela-Wooket Archery Camp, demonstrates good form in his *anchor*. (Photograph by D. Crowley, Jr.)

Fig. 2–8. Jim Hosford of Washington, D.C., veteran field archer and Teela-Wooket archery staff member, demonstrates his field *anchor*, a slight modification from those shown by Haugen and Thomas. (Photograph by D. Crowley, Jr.)

5. AIMING. An important point to remember in aiming is to concentrate your attention on the smallest spot you can see in the center of what you wish to hit. You may have heard the old saying, "You couldn't hit the broad side of a barn door." Actually it is possible for a beginning archer to miss a barn door. However, he would be much more likely to hit the door if he aimed to hit a small knothole in its middle than if he aimed at the door in general.

Field archery targets have small aiming spots in the center of their bull's-eyes. They are there for the distinct purpose of aiding archers to concentrate on the small aiming spot rather than shooting at the target in general.

a) Aiming in field and hunting archery is a combination of mental and muscular coordination. In explaining to beginners the essence of the bare-bow (instinctive) style of shooting, field archers commonly make such statements as "It's like shooting a pistol from the hip," "throwing a stone at a mark," or "shooting marbles"; you do not use any sighting gadgets. Similarly in field shooting, you just draw the bow back to your anchor, concentrate with *both* eyes open and look at the smallest spot that you can distinguish in the middle of the target, release, and follow through. This is what a good instinctive archer does, but how did he acquire the skill to do it that way? If he makes good scores on field archery ranges, and is a successful hunter, he has educated his bow arm and hand to hold the bow at the right place for whatever distance he needs to shoot. He probably developed this skill through months, and in some cases years, of careful practice. Certainly both the military archers of old and the American Indians learned to shoot this way. They shot every day from early boyhood. In this constant daily practice of shooting the bow and arrow regularly over the years, the Indian trained his bow arm to hold his bow at the right height to hit game, or his enemy, from whatever distance he needed to shoot. His accuracy was good considering the crude and inefficient weapons he had.

The object of this section of the book is to present suggestions that will shorten the process of educating (training) the bow arm and hand to hold the bow at the proper position. Nothing of course will take the place of practice, but it is important to practice with proper techniques. Practice with faulty techniques does more harm than good.

Good basic techniques are available for helping bare-bow field archers figure out how to hit the mark, regardless of distances involved. These techniques involve the pre-draw gap and post-draw gap systems for shooting.

The pre-draw gap system is useful at the shorter distances, and the post-draw gap from about 40 to 60 yards, or to that distance at which the gap has completely disappeared. As distance increases and the gap (post-draw) finally has disappeared, and the point of the arrow at full draw must be aimed on the target for a hit, then we have *point-blank* shooting.

It needs to be emphasized that the use of these gap systems is not to be regarded as an end in itself. They are but steps or means to the end—tools to more quickly educate (train) the bow arm of the archer. The goal is to enable the archer to more quickly arrive at the point where he can shoot bare-bow style automatically without having to lean on any gap system.

In the use of any gap system, the gap should be seen only indirectly, with peripheral rather than by direct vision. The archer should look with both eyes at the very spot he is trying to hit. His peripheral vision, noting the gap, tends to guide him in his early learning. When he has reached the point in his shooting where he is unaware of his use of a gap, he is probably shooting the field style automatically and correctly. Now let us consider details of the gap systems for shooting archery.

Pre-Draw Gap System.   The technique known as the pre-draw gap system * can be used as an aid to greatly speed training in bare-bow shooting at the shorter distances. It will help find the proper elevation for a hit at distances up to about 35 yards, a distance within which nearly all small-game and most big-game animals are bagged.

The interrelationships of the pre- and post-draw gap systems are illustrated in Figs. 2–9 and 2–10. Beginning field archers should start their shooting at short distances. Training with the *pre-draw* gap system of shooting should be started from a distance of 7 yards.

---

* This system was first explained to the authors by Mr. Dick Wilson of the Archery Division of Shakespear Company, Kalamazoo, Michigan, who called it the pre-gap system.

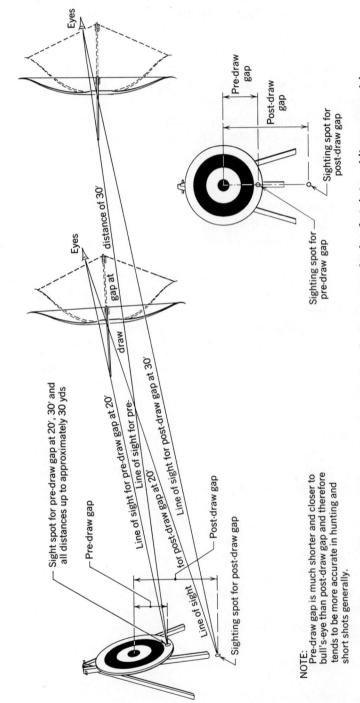

Sight spot for pre-draw gap at 20', 30' and all distances up to approximately 30 yds

Pre-draw gap

Line of sight for pre-draw gap at 20'
Line of sight for pre-

for post-draw gap at 20'
Line of sight for post-draw gap at 30'

Post-draw gap

Line of sight

Sighting spot for post-draw gap

Eyes

gap at draw

distance of 30'

Eyes

Pre-draw gap

Post-draw gap

Sighting spot for post-draw gap

Sighting spot for pre-draw gap

NOTE:
Pre-draw gap is much shorter and closer to bull's-eye than post-draw gap and therefore tends to be more accurate in hunting and short shots generally.

Fig. 2–9.   Comparison of the pre-draw and post-draw gap methods of sighting (diagrammatic).

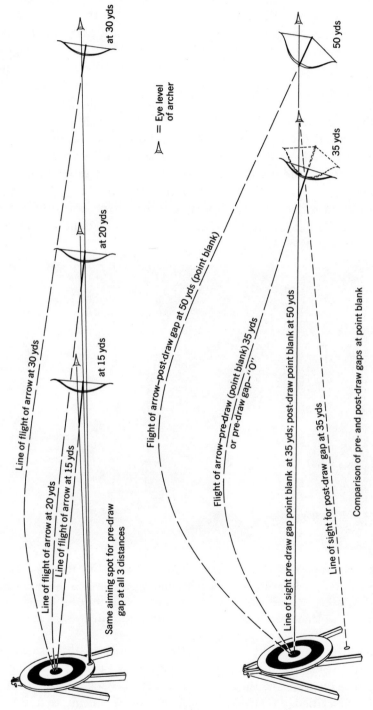

at 30 yds

50 yds

= Eye level
of archer

35 yds

at 20 yds

at 15 yds

Line of flight of arrow at 30 yds

Flight of arrow—post-draw gap at 50 yds (point blank)

Line of flight of arrow at 20 yds

Line of flight of arrow at 15 yds

Flight of arrow—pre-draw (point blank) 35 yds
or pre-draw gap—"0"

Same aiming spot for pre-draw
gap at all 3 distances

Line of sight pre-draw gap point blank at 35 yds; post-draw point blank at 50 yds

Line of sight for post-draw gap at 35 yds

Comparison of pre- and post-draw gaps at point blank

Fig. 2–10. Advantage of pre-draw gap system of aiming at the shorter distances (diagrammatic).

The archer should take the proper stance already described for field archery on page 10 (Fig. 2–1), except for the following: (1) the right shoulder is brought forward and the upper torso is turned to the left so that it faces the target, (2) the canted bow (about 20 degrees) and left arm are extended in proper position out toward the target (Fig. 2–3). Because the right shoulder is forward, one is able to reach forward with the right arm and take the proper grip on the bowstring (index finger is above the arrow and the other two fingers below it). The arrow and the right forearm should be kept in the same straight line at all times, with the right elbow at shoulder height. This and the next step all take place before the draw. Now with both eyes open, raise or lower the bow so that when looking down over the point of the arrow, the top of the point (pile) appears to be about 12 inches (or one diameter of a 12-inch field target face) below the bottom of the target. Be certain that the sighting is done across the point only, not down the length of the arrow. Remember this sighting is done before the draw (Figs. 2–11 and 2–12).

Fig. 2–11. Haugen demonstrates the *pre-draw aim*. His line of sight is indicated by the line from his eye through the top of the pile (head) of his arrow to a level possibly 12 inches below the target. Note that he is sighting across the tip, not down the length of the arrow. (Photograph by D. Crowley, Jr.)

Next, while keeping the bow arm (left) steadily in this aimed position, *shift the eyes* up to the aiming spot in the center of the target and concentrate on it. Then draw the string and arrow back to the field anchor previously described on page 16. This of course means that the fleshy V made by the thumb and index finger will be saddled behind the corner of

Fig. 2–12. Authors Haugen and Metcalf assist archer David Baier of Oreland, Pennsylvania, to learn the pre-draw gap system at Teela-Wooket. Note the string held at David's eye level to indicate his line of sight through the pile of his arrow to a white spot about 9 inches below the target. The distance between the spot and the target is the *pre-draw gap*. (Photograph by D. Crowley, Jr.)

the right jaw. The index finger will fit snugly under the cheekbone, and the tip of the index finger will rest about at the corner of the mouth. The head will be slightly tilted in keeping with the bow. All this time you must hold the bow at the level and place where you first aimed. From this position execute a live smooth release.

Shoot four or five arrows using the pre-draw aiming gap as above (one diameter of the 12-inch target face below the bottom of the target); note where the arrows group. They might all be in the bull's-eye or they might be consistently high or low. If the arrows hit high, increase the width of the pre-draw gap; and if the arrows are grouped low, decrease the gap by raising the bow and try again until you consistently hit in the middle. Then move back to 10 yards from the target and, using the same pre-draw gap as for 7 yards, shoot four arrows and see where they go. If they go low, raise the bow slightly (decreasing the pre-draw gap); and if high, lower it (increasing the gap); and eventually you will have adjusted your pre-draw gap to meet your personal need at the new distance. Remember to establish your aiming gap *before* you draw, then hold your bow there without letting it move while you shift your eyes to the "aiming spot," draw and shoot, even retaining the position during the afterhold. A modern 35-lb. bow of laminated glass construction may require approximately the same-sized pre-draw gap for all shooting distances from 7 to about 25 yards. This is a fortunate advantage in hunting.

Now let us review the steps. *One,* extend your bow with the undrawn arrow and elevate it to the position where you can see a gap of about one 12-inch target face below the target (if that is the proper pre-draw gap for the distance). *Two,* shift your eyes up to the aiming center in the middle of the target *without shifting the position of the bow arm in any way. Three,* draw the string and arrow back to the anchor without shifting the bow or arrow or bow arm from its original position at aim. *Four,* execute a good release in shooting the arrow from this position. The technique of the release will be dealt with later in this chapter.

Post-Draw Gap System. The post-draw gap system for shooting a bow is most effectively employed at the medium-long distances. Its usefulness starts at the longest distances of usefulness of the pre-draw gap. Where one leaves off, the other takes over. The post-draw gap is especially applicable in field archery rounds and for hunting big game in open country.

Except between the distances of 7 and about 25 yards where the gap changes very little, the pre-draw gap decreases as the distance from the target increases. Finally, at about 35 yards, the pre-draw gap has disappeared completely; and the pre-draw aim consists of sighting the arrow point, in the pre-draw position, directly onto the target (pre-draw-gap-0 [zero] or pre-draw point blank). If at this distance, a college coed using a moderate-quality solid-glass bow draws her bow while maintaining this bow-hand position, anchors, and then studies the *post-draw* position of the arrow point (before shooting), she will see that it appears to be far below the target. In fact, she will find a gap betwen the arrow point and the center of the target face. This is the *post-draw* gap. The gap may appear to be about two times as wide as the diameter of the target face (assuming she is shooting at an 18-inch face at this distance). At 40 yards, the post-draw gap may appear to have decreased to about one and one-half times the diameter of an 18-inch target face. The gap will continue to decrease as the distance increases until it is reduced to no gap at all at about 50 to 60 yards. This condition of point-on after draw, at whatever distance it occurs, is known as *point-blank range.* When the distance of shooting is greater than point-blank range, then the arrow tip must be held above the target. In other words, at distances longer than point-blank range, the condition becomes one of holding the arrow point higher and higher (more and more gap above the target) as the shooting distance increases.

For archers using the lower-priced type of equipment found in most physical education classes, the distances at which the post-draw gap appears above the target start at about 45 to 50 yards. An archer using a good 45-lb. laminated fiberglass bow may find the above-the-target gap appearing at about 60 yards.

The exact size of the gap is an individual proposition, and each archer must learn the gap or gaps related to his or her tackle and anchor. This can be learned only through experience.

Knowing all these relationships makes it possible not only to make a more accurate shot with the first arrow, but also to correct the elevation if the first one misses. It is a way to learn and establish good elevation habits for the bow hand.

b) Holding is an important and integral part of effective aiming. You must hold the full draw at anchor momentarily (2 or 3 seconds) to steady yourself before shooting. In hunting, the hold may be barely perceptible because the hunter sometimes must shoot fast. However, always come back to a full draw and anchor in order that each arrow will receive the power of a full draw. Snap-shooting is not good archery, but it may be necessary for a fleeting shot at a moving target. An arrow that is not shot from full draw is likely to fall short of its intended mark; or if it hits game, it may result in an ineffective hit. Shoot as fast as you must, but do so only with full control, and be sure to take a full draw and anchor with every shot.

6. RELEASE. The release is the sixth basic fundamental of archery technique. For a proper release, it is important that the fingers, hand, wrist, forearm, and elbow all be in straight alignment with the arrow shaft during the draw and in the anchor position. This straight-line position must be maintained during and immediately after the release. With the bowstring suddenly leaving the fingertips of the right hand as a result of relaxing the flexed fingers, and with the shoulder muscles continuing to pull the elbow backward, it is inevitable that the entire right arm unit (upper arm, elbow, forearm, wrist, hand, and fingers) will spring backward. During this movement backward, the right elbow starts to move back and out of the previous straight line and tends toward a position behind the archer's back. This is so since the arm being attached at the shoulder joint cannot continue retreating in the same straight line it was in at anchor, but has to circle behind, the elbow scribing a circular movement backward with the upper arm being the radius of the movement. As the backward movement starts, the elbow circling behind it is followed first by the forearm and then by the wrist. The hand and fingers, however, must *not* be allowed to circle, but must continue straight backward along the original line of the arrow as it was at anchor. This will necessitate a slight inward bend of the right wrist, allowing the fingers to lightly brush the neck or side of the face on their way straight back from the anchor.

One must concentrate on the fingers brushing the neck or the side of the face to keep all motion in the line of the arrow although moving in exactly the opposite direction. Any variation from this "in-line-with-the-arrow" release will cause the arrows shot to disperse rather than to group together.

Plucking is a common fault in the release of arrows. This is where the fingers and hand pull off and away from the face at the moment of release. Plucking, and other variations causing dispersion of the arrows at release, can be avoided by keeping the hand and fingers in the same planes (both vertical and horizontal) as the arrow at anchor, and having the fingers brush the neck during the *natural* backward recoil of the right arm following release. The word natural is stressed because some archers observing the backward recoiling release movements (live release) of skilled archers mimic the motion but do so as an afterthought, after the instantaneous recoil is over. The backward movement from the anchor position must be one that flows naturally as a part of the recoil (not an afterthought).

What makes a live release live, how is it accomplished, and what muscles are involved? The expression *live release* aptly describes a good release in which the natural flowing action of the right arm and its parts during recoil are visibly evident as one continuous movement. A dead release is one in which only the shooting fingers are involved in the action. The fingers simply extend, finally releasing the string 1 to 1½ inches in front of the anchor point, thus losing at least an inch of the draw, with a loss of power of the bow. Furthermore, in a dead release, muscles come into play that are antagonistic to those responsible for the natural backward movement during recoil.

In drawing the arrow back to the anchor, the muscles that should be used are those that pull the right shoulder blade toward the spine (middle sections of the trapezius) and those that draw the right arm toward the shoulder blade (posterior deltoid, infra-spinatus, and teres minor). The middle deltoid muscle, which goes over the top of the shoulder joint, also contracts to keep the elbow at the right height. The other important muscles used (flexor profundus digitorum) flex the first joint of the fingers so that they can be hooked onto the string. All other muscles should be kept relatively relaxed so that there can be a straight line of pull from the bent fingertips to the elbow. Incidentally, the contracting of other finger (fist) and wrist muscles at this time is what throws the arrow off the arrow-rest and interferes with the essential straight-line pull.

Creeping is a fault an archer must avoid. It means that the pile and foreshaft of the arrow are allowed to creep slowly forward to some point ahead of where it was originally drawn. It results in loss of effective length of draw and usually occurs without the archer being aware of it. A creeping arrow always falls low or short of where it was intended to go.

In order to maintain the anchor steadfastly during the process of aiming and holding, without "creeping," the same muscles as those used in the draw (described above) must be used continuously and with increasing vigor. While aiming and holding, the archer must increase his concentration on continuing the force of the draw. It becomes a conscious effort to keep on using the muscles between the right shoulder blade and the spine, and between the upper arm and the shoulder blade. The archer must concentrate on continuing to force the elbow of his drawing arm backward, backward, backward from the target. This is the secondary draw. It is the second and final emphasis on the contraction of the muscles back of the right shoulder. This increasing contraction of these muscles should continue throughout aiming and holding until after the instant of release when the fingertips relax, letting the string shoot the arrow forward. The builtup pressure in the shoulder muscles, being released, causes the backward rebound or recoil previously discussed.

In shooting a rifle, one holds on the mark, squeezes the trigger, and does not know exactly when the gun will discharge. So in archery one aims and holds on the mark, meanwhile concentrating on "squeezing" the right shoulder closer and closer to the spine until the hold is steady on the mark and the eyes agree it is time for the fingers to relax and let the string go. If there is sufficient concentration on using the muscles behind the right shoulder, and all other muscles of the right arm unit are relaxed except for the muscles controlling the hooking of the fingertips, a good, smooth, and live release will result.

Reiterated emphases on the use of the muscles back of the right shoulder are unnecessary for the *good, experienced* archer who does the right things automatically. The beginning archer, however, or an archer who is having trouble with the release, should study and practice the secondary draw conscientiously.

An alert beginner, when told to keep bringing the elbow back and to use the back shoulder muscles, may ask whether that will not overdraw the arrow and perhaps bring the hand back beyond the proper anchor.

To prevent overdraw, the bowstring immediately above the right index finger may be arrested by contact with the right cheekbone, and against the middle of the right eyeglass if such are used. Another possible check against overdraw is to draw (with back and shoulder muscles) the joint of the base of the right index finger snugly and tightly against the muscle (masseter muscle) that closes the jaws on the right-hand side. Each archer should use the overdraw check that works best for him.

A check against overdrawing when using the modified field anchor (Fig. 2–8) consists of drawing the second joint of the right thumb tighter against the rear boundary of the depression behind the right jaw (forward surface of the base of the mastoid bone where the sterno-mastoid muscle is attached). The drawing or pulling referred to in each case means the strong use of the muscles back of the right shoulder. One can concentrate on these back and shoulder muscles *only* (1) when the other muscles of the right arm, wrist, and fingers are *relaxed*, except for *slight* contraction of the muscle (right flexor profundis digitorum) flexing the outermost joints of the three string fingers, which are hooked over the string; and (2) when the straight-line (arrow, fingers, wrist, and elbow are all in a straight line in all planes) pull is maintained.

In order to become conscious of the "feel" of these back and shoulder muscles preliminary to a good release in field archery, a special exercise is suggested. It is employed by Mr. Jim Hosford, one of the best technicians in the "how" of shooting bare-bow style with the modified anchor. Hosford suggests coming back to the anchor, then creeping forward a fraction of an inch or so, then pulling back tight to the anchor and against the anchor overdraw check (whichever one is used), then relaxing the draw a little and pulling back once more to a tight snug anchor. Repeating this process three or four times always concentrating on the use of the back and shoulder muscles in pulling and holding snug at the anchor will help get the "feel."

An improvised method of getting the feel of this group of muscles and to strengthen them is to cut 1 to 1½ inch wide rubber bands from an old auto tire inner tube, and loop three of these together square-knot style like links of a chain (Fig. A–14, page 185). Place the far end of the loop at one end around the base of the left thumb as though it were a bow handle. Place the other end of the rubber chain over and about 2 or 3 inches above the right elbow (bent as in the drawing position). Hold the left arm in exactly the same position in which you would hold the bow and draw the elbow back so that the right hand can come back to your anchor and a little beyond. Then let up the pressure and allow the rubber bands to shorten to their normal position.

Repeat this exercise over and over until the proper muscles behind the right shoulder become tired. Remember the number of times you stretched the bands, and each day do the exercise more times than you did the previous day. While drawing the bands back, concentrate on the feel of using these back muscles.

Another means of strengthening these back muscles consists of hooking the fingertips of each hand together under the chin and then pulling the elbows outward (strong adduction of the shoulder blades) as hard as you can for a full 10 seconds. Doing this once a day will do wonders for strengthening your shoulder muscles.

7. AFTERHOLD OR FOLLOW-THROUGH. The *afterhold* or *follow-through* is the seventh and last basic fundamental of shooting the bow and arrow. It is exceedingly important for accuracy. An attempt has been made to show how each principle follows after the previous one in a particular and proper sequence.

At the end of the *release,* your bow and bow hand should still point directly at the target. The fingers of the hand that drew and released the string should have brushed the side of the face or neck and still (hand and fingers) be in the same straight line that the arrow was in before it left the string.

To properly execute the *afterhold,* the archer simply keeps both arms, the bow arm and the drawing arm, in the exact position they were in at the end of the release, and does so until the arrow has hit. Many beginning archers neglect the afterhold and at the instant of release, drop the bow arm down from its horizontal position, snap the right hand and arm downwards or down to the right, or move either or both arms in some other way.

Without the use of the afterhold, an archer may well have wasted all the time, precision, and care spent in properly executing all of the previous six fundamentals and their various steps. All six previous fundamentals may have been performed perfectly, and still that effort will have been wasted by dropping the bow arm and/or snapping away the string hand and arm at the instant after release. In this connection, students sometimes are humorously admonished with a statement like, "Let's not have all your good conscientious efforts in the six previous steps spoiled by a 'jerk.'"

A good afterhold many times makes the difference between hitting the bull's-eye or missing the target (Fig. 2–13). In hunting, neglecting the afterhold often means getting no game.

Fig. 2–13. Miss Haugen demonstrates the last of the seven basic fundamentals, the *afterhold* or *follow-through.* The arrow has gone, but both arms remain up in the position they were in when the arrow was released, except that the left hand and fingers, due to recoil, have brushed backward about 2 inches from their original position at anchor.

In deer hunting with bow and arrow, for example, neglecting the after-hold not only tends to throw the arrow wide of the deer, but the motion of dropping or waving the arms suddenly may scare the deer away.

To summarize, the seven basic fundamentals of shooting the bow and arrow have been presented in their proper sequence. The similarities and differences in the execution of these principles have been explained as they apply to field archery. Although the accomplished archer shoots with a smooth, efficient, and continuous flow of action from stance to afterhold, the beginner or the archer desiring to check his form must perform each fundamental and its various parts deliberately and in proper sequence. One must do it correctly before it can become automatic. Finally, great emphasis has been placed on proper use of the muscles that pull the shoulder blade back toward the spine and those that pull the arm back toward the shoulder blade. This muscular action is essential from the start of the draw through the anchor and the release. Relaxation comes at the instant of release with the *straight-in-line* movement of rebound or recoil as the fingers brush the side of the face or neck and the afterhold occurs.

3

Archery Golf and Other Field Archery Games

Archery golf played an important role in the development of an increasing interest in archery during the decade of 1930–1940. It gave target archers a most enjoyable and informal outlet not previously available to them. It was well adapted to informal participation in twosomes, threesomes, and foursomes as in golf and was particularly well suited for tournament competition. Target archers with leanings toward less formal types of shooting welcomed this game that emphasized each of the skills required in the usual events shot in the National Archery Association tournaments, but with more variety and freedom. It involves flight for distance, clout, and target shooting. Archery golf provides both recreation and enjoyment. It provides excellent opportunity for informal companionship.

Archery golf was also welcomed by bowhunters because it provided additional opportunities to practice judging distances and to do roving while using the instinctive or bare-bow style of shooting.

In golf one drives from the tee and fairway for distance, makes an approach to the green, and then "holes out" by putting. In archery golf one shoots a flight arrow from behind the tee-marker for distance; perhaps takes another flight shot for distance (from the spot where his first arrow landed) if still necessary; makes an approach to the target by shooting a "roving" or "field" arrow (often with a longer more pointed steel point to prevent the arrow's skidding); and then continues shooting until the bull's-eye, a soft, white rubber ball 4 inches in diameter, is hit. As in golf, the person taking the fewest strokes wins; so in archery golf, the person using the fewest shots to hit all the balls wins.

Like the Field Archery Round (the official game of the National Field Archery Association), archery golf could claim its origin from early (1300–1590) military requirements of males in England to spend a certain number of hours daily shooting at the butts and over roving courses several miles long. Actually, however, organized archery golf was the immediate forerunner of the field archery round; and "Bonarro" was the immediate predecessor of organized archery golf. The idea of archery golf was thought of, demonstrated, and occasionally played informally by a number of archers previous to World War I; but it did not reach a stage of organization for large-scale competition until the 1920's. Ohio was an early stronghold for archery golf.

RECOMMENDED ARCHERY GOLF GAME

Archery golf as it is played at the Teela-Wooket Archery Camp, Roxbury, Vermont, is both simple and inexpensive. It involves the use of soft white rubber balls 4 inches in diameter for targets. These are supported on wire loops made from No. 9 soft iron wire, or wire coat hangers. To make an archery golf target, cut the wire into 34-inch lengths. Sharpen one end of a 34-inch piece and measure 6 inches up from the pointed end; wrap a 2-inch length of 1½-inch adhesive tape tightly around the wire at this point. Eighteen inches from the bottom of the tap, bend the upper end of the wire at right angles and curl or bend it into a circle not over 3 inches in diameter. Stick the lower 6 inches of the wire vertically into the ground as far as the adhesive tape (which acts as a stopper) and place the rubber ball on the wire circle, which will support it 18 inches above the ground (Fig. 3–1).

Place nine or eighteen of these ball-on-wire targets just off to the sides of

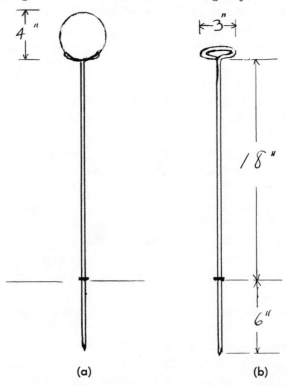

(a)   (b)

Fig. 3–1. Archery golf target: (a) a 4-inch ball balanced on top of a wire loop and (b) the wire support for the ball.

the greens of a nine- or eighteen-hole golf course, and the course is set. Archery golf can be adapted to the space available by playing with fewer than nine targets. The archery golf course at the National Archery Camp, at Teela-Wooket, is a six-target course. Note the sample score card of the six-target archery golf course of the Teela-Wooket Archery Camp on page 37, and some types of arrows used (Fig. 3–2), and note also the illustrations of archery golf at this camp (Figs. 3–3 and 3–4).

In playing the game, one simply starts from behind the tee-marker and shoots toward the target, counting each shot taken until the ball has been hit and knocked off the wire support. If on a previous shot the arrow lies so close to the target that when the archer stands with both feet behind the point of this arrow he can touch the ball on its wire support with the pile of another arrow nocked on the bow string, it is conceded that the ball could be shot off the wire on the next shot. Therefore, one point is automatically added to the score and the shot need not be made.

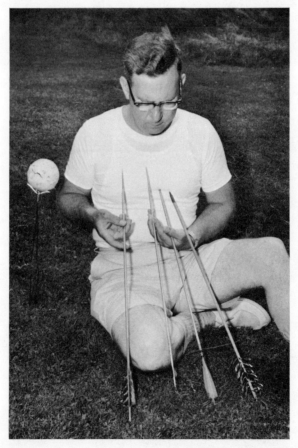

Fig. 3–2. Some types of archery golf arrows are shown by Charles Pierson, former national flight champion from Cincinnati, Ohio. Arrows shown (from left to right) are spike-pointed, non-skid arrow for hard ground; flight arrow for distance; non-skid for use on ice; and flu flu "putting" arrow.

Fig. 3–3. Archery golf is a fine family sport. Metcalf is shown "holing out" (shooting out) following a good approach shot.

Fig. 3–4. Mrs. Harlan Metcalf and Mrs. Arnold Haugen "tee off" in archery golf at the Teela-Wooket Archery Camp's scenic course at Roxbury, Vermont.

SIX-TARGET
ARCHERY GOLF COURSE
SCORE CARD

Targets	Yards	Par	Players Names			
1	200	3				
2	224	3				
3	100	2				
4	153	2				
5	93	2				
6	187	3				
	957	15				

SAFETY FIRST ALWAYS

Bows and arrows can be dangerous. AVOID any possible danger to archers and all others on or about the course.

Take the TEE SHOT only AFTER archers have left the green ahead of you.

Proceed only AFTER everyone in the group has shot his arrow.

Following are the rules for archery golf as played at the Teela-Wooket Archery Camp.

RULES FOR ARCHERY GOLF

OBJECT OF GAME: To knock a 4-inch diameter ball off a stand which is 18 inches tall.

Each group shall select a captain to make decisions and to record scores AFTER leaving EACH green.

Only ONE BOW may be used unless it is broken, in which case the shot may be taken over with another bow without penalty. The same applies to a broken bow string.

Arrows of any kind may be used.

Each shot counts ONE, also each penalty.

The stand for a field shot, which may be a flight or approach shot, must be directly behind the point of landing of the previous shot.

The archer with the lowest score on each target shoots first on the next tee shot.

After the tee shot the archer farthest from the target shoots first. DO NOT AD-VANCE UNTIL THE SHOT IS COMPLETED. All archers remain on line with the archer shooting, or behind him—NEVER at any point between shooter and the target even at extreme right or left.

Full draw is not required. The bow may be held in any position.

An arrow in an unplayable position may be shot from a point at equal or greater distance from the target, with a penalty of one point added.

A lost arrow if not found in 5 minutes may be replaced by another which is shot from a spot agreed upon by the group, with a penalty of one point added.

A shot may be conceded with one point added to the score if an arrow lands near enough to the target so that the archer can make the point of his NOCKED arrow touch the target. The FEET must remain in their stand behind the spot where the POINT of the previously shot arrow landed.

"FAST" is the term used if it is necessary to signal anyone on the course.

In case of a TIE there shall be a play off.

ARCHERY ETIQUETTE

"Do unto others as you would have them do unto you"—always.

OTHER FIELD ARCHERY GAMES

Some of the following games can be played in class as possible substitutes for one or more games that are listed as part of the twenty-five lessons in Appendix A; others are best for small groups on special occasions. All can be easily adapted to camp, club, or forest recreation programs.

ROVING. Although this game is most often played in a small informal group of two to five archers, it can be enjoyed by a class of twenty-four or more students if properly organized. Such a class should be divided into groups, each containing not more than six persons. Each group must play at a safe distance from any other group. Ordinary pasture land or open wooded areas are best, and permission from the owner of the land should be secured before using it.

A shooting order for all members of a group is established, giving each team member in their turn the right, first, to choose the target at which all in the small group must shoot and, second, the privilege of shooting first. Each person in the team shoots only one arrow at the target specified. Anyone hitting the target scores 5 points. Of those missing the target (which might include all the members of the team or group), the person whose arrow comes closest to the target scores 3 points, the next closest arrow scores 2 points, and the next closest 1 point, and the other arrows no points.

Suitable marks for roving would be a rotten tree stump at 20–30 yards, a dandelion at 5–15 yards, a bare spot on the ground at 30–50 yards, a piece of bark at 20 yards, a bush or shrub at 100 yards, or a leaf at 10 yards. In the selection of a target, care must be taken to choose one that if hit will not ruin the arrow. The background of the target should be soft earth or sand that will not damage the arrows. However, it is expected that a few arrows may get lost or broken; so all players should carry extra ones. Obviously, all should shoot their one arrow at the particular target before anyone advances to see where his arrow has hit. Finding your arrow quickly after each shot provides more opportunity for shooting and adds to the enjoyment of the game. To facilitate quick finding, always note the exact spot from which you shot and keep your eye on the spot the arrow appeared to hit until you can walk directly there and pick it up. Do not be tempted to shoot two arrows at the same target in roving. To do so may cost you the loss of an arrow. You can concentrate only on where one lands.

Other games for field archers are listed in the *Official Handbook of Field Archery*.* Try one of the following:

William Tell Shoot
Rabbit Hunt Tournament
Low Man's Choice
Hit and Drop Back
Reduction Tournament
April Fool Tournament
The Stump Round
The Redland's Round

Try the latter one on an Operation Archery Modified Flint Round course. This can be done on your school course whether indoors or outdoors, and will add interest and variety to the school or club program.

---

* *Official Handbook of Field Archery* (11th ed.; Redlands, Calif.: National Field Archery Association of the U.S.A., 1961).

4

Laying Out the Field Course

There are many followers of field archery who regard field shooting as nothing but practice for hunting. This concept is only partially true. It is too narrow and restrictive. Field shooting can establish good form and automatic shooting habits. It should produce an educated bow hand that can act with a minimum of conscious help on your part when a quick running shot is the best you can get, or when buck fever strikes.

With carelessness, field shooting can also establish poor shooting habits. However, even with good shooting form and habits, there is much to be learned about hunting that can be learned only by hunting experience. Experience is a dear teacher, yet many tricks in hunting can be learned in no other way. Since the fun of hunting is in the chase, who would want to learn by any other means? The art of outsmarting a deer cannot be learned on a field course or entirely out of a book. If you are one of those who believe it can be done that way, you will probably return from your next hunt *a sadder and wiser huntsman,* but with no meat for the pan.

A PHILOSOPHY ON FIELD COURSES

If field archery is to be given the opportunity to provide the many pleasures with which the game is endowed, considerable planning must go into laying out each course. It must include the philosophy of "outdoor fun in more ways than one." First and foremost, *the course must be pleasant to shoot.* It should take advantage of the lay of the land for a challenging layout and, where possible, offer banks or sloping ground to catch stray arrows. Rocks, and trees that stand immediately behind the target or crowd the shooting lanes too closely, thereby being hazards to arrows that narrowly miss targets, should be avoided as far as possible.

The beginning archer is very sensitive to unnecessary loss or breakage of his arrows. Unnecessary hazards have discouraged and driven away hundreds, yes thousands, of beginners in years past. This is unfortunate because the very life of every club is dependent upon beginners. This is especially true because of the rapid turnover in membership in almost every club. In one state association in the Midwest, only a very few archers were still competing after a 5-year period. Everything possible should be done to

Fig. 4–1. Part of the fun in field archery comes from shooting on a pleasant and interesting field course. This scene on the 80-yard target layout at the First National Tournament shows Eugene Little of Michigan and Hewitt Gall of Wisconsin competing. (Photograph by W. Leon Riegler.)

Fig. 4–2. A blanket of snow on any field course adds beauty to the scenery as well as a new challenge to your shooting ability. Here "Nita" Haugen is enjoying the Swan Creek Field Course (Allegan, Michigan), the first Conservation Department–sponsored course in the nation.

make life pleasant for the beginner; he is the future backbone of any club. Without him the club will go "broke" and out of existence.

Whenever possible, courses should be laid out so as to take full advantage of the beauty of the landscape. Absolute safety in the layout must also be given careful consideration. No official should approve any course unless it is absolutely safe. The welfare and future of field archery depends on keeping the sport safe on every course.

Courses laid out with the foot paths up and down steep slopes as if they were meant to be obstacle courses for mountain goats are acceptable only to "young bucks" and some "old experts." If an archer must feel all worn out at the end of the day, let it be from shooting, not from unnecessary climbing up and down steep banks and hills. This does not mean that all hills are to be avoided; it merely means using discretion in how paths and target positions are laid out. Use the sense of our American bison (buffalo) in path-making. These wise prairie animals ambled into the hills too; but when they did so, their paths were in easy grades along or around slopes. Pioneer wagon trails, and the railroads that followed, commonly paralleled these trails because their grades were gradual and easy to travel. Let us follow the lead of the bison and make our trails easy and pleasant to travel. Field archery should be enjoyable to everyone from beginner to champion, and for young and older bowmen alike. It should offer real opportunity for family fun (Fig. 4–3). To lay out a course that suits archers of all ages takes real imagination and planning. It means getting the most out of the terrain for the course.

YOUR FIELD ARCHERY GROUNDS

As many archers have learned, it is not always easy to find a piece of ground suitable for a good field archery course, especially where it will be convenient, yet far enough afield to minimize vandalism. It is seldom that permission can be secured to lay out such a course in a city park; and when and if established in such a crowded area, problems with vandalism and/or safety are usually considerable. With the public wandering around at random and with many non-archers convinced that they have as much right on the course as you have, conditions can become outright dangerous to the wanderer and unnerving to the archer. Under such conditions there is little enjoyment in shooting. If and when a field course is established in a park, authorities should be requested to restrict the use of that area to archery only, and to post it accordingly.

Wooded parcels of land, preferably with short slopes, ravines, or small hills, and outside of town, seem most appropriate for field archery. It will require roughly 10 acres of land for each 14-target course unless the terrain is very suitable. The area may be available without charge from a club member, a public-spirited citizen, or more probably may be leased at some

Fig. 4–3. Field archery is a fine family recreational activity. There is a class for competition for everyone from young to old. The family noon-day picnic in the shade of a sheltering tree adds much to the occasion. Pictured is the Haugen family: Arnold, Chris, "Nita," Arnold Orland, Sonja, and Sallie. (Photograph courtesy of Auburn University.)

specified fee. A lease with all conditions for use and responsibilities stipulated will help minimize chances for misunderstanding or disagreement. In certain areas, state or federal land may be available for a course.

Over the years, clubs will be stronger if they own the land on which they shoot. Club grounds may be secured through purchase, donation, or may be willed to the club by some public-spirited citizen. One club raised the money to purchase a plot of land by selling interest-bearing shares to its members. These shares are being paid off through money-raising ventures, dues, and tournament profits. The arrangement has worked well and has given the club a place of its own with a maximum of security. Improvements at the field course include a headquarters building, a deep-well pump, latrines, and electric lights. Their club's investment is further "sweetened" by the fact that deer roam the range. Members hunt them in season. A growing stand of good hardwood timber on the acreage is increasing the value of the property each year.

Not enough effort has been made to appeal to financially independent individuals to underwrite field courses on the local level. Here there is a chance to provide public recreation, a means for providing physical fitness, and the possibility for constructive leadership in youth activity all rolled into one sport. It would seem that such a possibility could be "sold" to some citizen or company blessed with enough earning power to be in the upper income tax bracket. By incorporating as a non-profit corporation, some of that money might be acquired for expansion.

Another source that may add to the financing of clubs and help make land available is the fact that field archery has now been in existence long enough so that older members of years gone by may wish to provide for field archery in their wills.

LAYING OUT YOUR FIELD COURSE

Once you have arranged for a suitable area for your field course, try your best to locate a central location for headquarters. The site should be large enough to permit parking the participants' cars, even on a tournament day, and to accommodate a fenced play area for children. It should include shade for resting and picnicking and have a suitable assembly spot for registration and for presenting awards. The necessity for the provision of respectable sanitary facilities is obvious.

The headquarters area must be entirely safe with adequate room for at least three practice butts per 14-target unit to be laid out. There must be no shooting toward the headquarters area unless the target is at least 100 yards distant or unless a suitable hill intervenes to protect the area from glancing arrows.

It is most desirable to have the course or courses clover-leaf out from the staging area so that targets 1 and 14 of each unit are nearest the starting point. For beginning or small clubs, each clover-leaf loop should probably consist of a 14-target unit. Large clubs may wish to lay out two or three 28-target courses, with targets 1 and 28 of each course nearest the starting point.

For convenience and for properly laying out a course and to get the most out of the terrain, you will need about thirty strips of colored rags (about 2" × 18", any color) and a similar number of white ones. Include a pencil and a notebook in your paraphernalia.

Before you place a single rag, scout the entire area, making mental notes of layout possibilities. The second time you start out from the selected headquarters area, you may start marking the prospective positions.

Pick a safe and convenient spot for the first target. Place a colored rag on a bush, limb of a tree, or a stick to indicate the possible shooting position; then put up a white rag at the prospective target-bale position. Do not place any stakes at the bale or shooting position yet. Just pace the distance and record the target number and its prospective distance in yards. Also, indicate the possible minimum and maximum distances for the target in case a change is needed. Now go on to target position 2 and do the same, but try to select a distance that is still needed for the course. Repeat this procedure until all the required distances have been marked for an official N.F.A.A. regulation 14-target unit.

A standard 14-target field round unit as defined by the official N.F.A.A. handbook consists of the following 14 targets:*

15-, 20-, 25-, and 30-yard targets, each with a 12-inch face (four arrows at each distance)

40-, 45-, and 50-yard targets, each with an 18-inch face (four arrows at each distance)

55-, 60-, and 65-yard targets, each with a 24-inch face (four arrows at each distance)

and the following four-position shots (each arrow to be shot from a different position or at a different target):

30-35-40-45 yards with an 18-inch face
35 yards with an 18-inch face and each arrow shot from a different angle
50-60-70-80 yards with a 24-inch face
20-25-30-35 feet at a 6-inch face or faces

Now examine your note pad. Have the distances been well mixed with alternating shorter and longer target distances to permit interesting shooting? Do your notes indicate you can switch some of the target distances around to advantage to make the layout more challenging? Now walk back over the area once more and change the positions of the rags where such will improve your course. Be absolutely certain that the layout is safe. A distance of at least 25 yards should separate the target bales of each target from the shooting position for another. In no case should the next shooting position or butt be behind or in line with the direction of shooting on another target.

If after all angles have been considered, you feel you have gotten the most out of the site, you are now ready to carry in the bales of straw to the target positions. Marsh hay, excelsior, and wheat straw are good for backstops or butts because they are quite resistant to deterioration if they get wet. Oat straw and alfalfa hay are inferior in lasting quality because they decay rapidly after becoming wet. Pick the exact target spot to take advantage of any rise in ground to stop stray arrows. Leveling the target spot and placing an old automobile tire casing under the bales will keep them off the ground and help keep out moisture (Fig. 4–4). If the casing is a thin one and has a tendency to collapse as a result of the weight of the bales,

* *Official Handbook of Field Archery* (11th ed.; Redlands, Calif.: National Field Archery Association of the U.S.A., 1961).

Fig. 4–4. Note the tire casing supporting the target butt, keeping the bottom bale off the ground and dry. A piece of roofing paper held in place with a few shovelfuls of dirt keeps the top bale protected from wetting by rains. Here a boy scout aims at the mark. Field archery is recognized as a merit badge accomplishment in scouting.

put a stick of wood about 4 inches in diameter across the center of the tire with the ends protruding into the casing. Cut a hole into the bottom side of the tire so that it cannot hold water and thereby become a mosquito-breeding haven.

To prevent the bales coming apart prematurely due to rusting and breaking of the original baling wires or twine, all bales should be tightly rebound with No. 9 galvanized wire (Fig. 4–5). Banding the bales together with a steel strip as used in some machines that put bands around crates or boxes also works well. Where two or three bales are used for a single target butt, wire or band them together as a single unit. To reduce chances for pass-through arrows at the juncture of the bales, pack a piece of ordinary gunny-sack material between the bales before binding them together. To provide a target butt that will stop most near-miss arrows and thereby encourage the average archer, it is recommended that clubs use four-bale butts for the 24-inch faces, three-bale butts for 18-inch, and two-bale butts for 12- and 6-inch faces.

Fig. 4–5. Bales of hay or straw used for field archery target butts should be rebound with No. 9 galvanized wire. A tightening gadget made from two pieces of 1½-foot long ¾-inch pipe and an elbow serves well for tightening the wire. A small hole in the side of the pipe serves to catch and hold the end of the wire after it is threaded through an eye on the other end of the wire. The pipe is twisted to pull the wire tight.

Place the target butt on the tire casing and secure the bales to two husky stakes driven into the ground on the back side to hold it upright. Be sure the stakes do not project above the bales and thereby serve as hazards to arrows. If you fasten the butt to the stakes with No. 9 wire and cut the ends short, no wayward individual will be able to untwist the wire with his bare hands to tear the target down.

To keep rain from soaking the bales, they may be covered with water-proof materials such as "sisalcraft," plastic sheets, or truck-sized inner tubes (split open). Any of these materials should be applied before banding so that the wires will hold the cover in place. Tarred paper rainproof covering may be put on top of the completed bale and then held in place with a few shovelfuls of dirt. A good plastic cover will keep the bale dry and in good condition for a much longer period and thereby reduce maintenance problems.

A properly placed butt is one whose entire target face is visible from the shooting position, even to the littlest archers.

You should now use a tape measure to measure the distances from the targets to the shooting positions and set the shooting stakes at the appropriate positions. Until 1962, a 5 per cent variation in distance from the regular required distance for any target was permitted where necessary because of terrain. Now, however, each of the 14 target distances for an official course must be exactly as specified for the standard round. The distances are considered as line-of-sight distances.

Plan for two separate shooting stakes or shooting lanes to each target. On the four-position targets, you will need four stakes. Be sure the stakes and shooting lanes on the four-position targets are so arranged that it is absolutely safe for two archers to shoot simultaneously. The shots, however, should not be spread sideways to such an extent that the arrows hitting the target will strike each other from wide side angles and result in excessive breakage.

By laying out your course so that two archers at a time can safely and conveniently shoot at each target, you will eliminate a lot of delays in tournaments and add interest to the layout of the course.

The next operation will be to lay out the footpaths. For the most sporting as well as the most scenic layout, the trails should curve to the side and, where possible, follow the contour of the ground to the target. Paths leading directly from the shooting stakes to the target distract from the naturalness of the area and may make the course easier to shoot. Curve the paths enough so that the line of flight of the arrow will be over natural vegetation, gullies, water, and so forth.

It takes a lot of experience to determine how much a path can be detoured and still get the archers to use it. If the path is too circuitous, the shooters make their own new trail, even over bushes, boulders, or small brush heaps in order to go directly to the target. Be sure to make the path easy to travel, even for the old and tired.

The next operation will be to brush out and rake leaves and stones from in front of and from behind the targets, and to clear a respectable-sized shooting lane. Cut no wider a shooting lane than necessary, but allow for the high trajectory of 20- to 25-lb. bows, which are commonly used by women, juniors, and some beginners. Keep the lane as natural as possible, but allow ample room for a reasonably well-shot arrow to land safely on or near the target.

Providing an occasional "sitting" log at shooting positions does much to add comfort and enjoyment to shooting. Tin-can ashtrays at the shooting stakes may help reduce fire hazard. One fire may turn the whole setup to ashes and your efforts to naught in a matter of minutes.

Some clubs improvise bow racks at the target butts and shooting positions by cutting off the tips of limbs on a sapling or small tree so that short stiff stubs about 6 inches long remain. All these finer points help add fun to the game.

The N.F.A.A. in 1962 altered its constitution to permit archery *clubs* to mark the actual shooting distance on each of the shooting stakes on their field, hunters, fixed distance handicap, and park rounds. It was left to the discretion of each club to do as it wished whether to mark or not to mark the distances. The marking of shooting distances, especially for the field and hunters rounds, is a drastic deviation from the original intent and tradition of field archery. It is a move toward "targetizing" field archery, which, if it continues, will take a lot of fun out of field shooting for the average bare-bow archer; and he is the archer who built field archery. Part of the fun in bare-bow field shooting comes from the opportunity to estimate shooting distances to the various targets. That is part of the game, just as it is in hunting. Remove this challenge and you have weakened the bond between field and hunting archery (Fig. 4–6).

Fig. 4–6. Four typical "bare-bow" archers at the 1961 Iowa State Championship Field Archery Tournament. With little hope for winning the meet, they were there because they enjoyed the shooting and the genial fellowship.

In the long run, it would seem wiser to keep rounds of the type most *enjoyed* by Mr. Average Archer-Bowhunter, rather than the type of rounds demanded by those who shoot mainly for awards. Award-happy individuals have been known to "slip" around courses at night to measure target distances to secure an advantage over or to get even with competitors who may have done likewise in order to win State or National tournaments. Is this sportsmanship? Such individuals are more to be pitied than to be condemned.

Maintenance on courses is an important consideration. Some clubs have solved this problem by assigning a particular target to a member or a family. A spirit of friendly competition then develops and each attempts to make his or their target the best by providing bow racks, benches, ashtrays made of tin cans, and improved paths. They also strive to do a good job of raking stones, leaves, and other debris away from the target. Particular attention is paid to removing overhanging branches that might deflect arrows with high trajectories. When needed, the target bales are retightened or replaced. Such maintenance is good management and will contribute to a thriving club. Good maintenance is an absolute must. Without it, neither the club nor the course will last long.

The transporting of bales to the target positions on the course is usually a formidable task. This burden can be lightened considerably through the use of an L. L. Bean-type deer carrier. The carrier amounts to a sort of rigid stretcher mounted on a centrally located single bicycle-type wheel. The making of such a vehicle is no great task to a handyman. If stored at the clubhouse, it might even be of use in bringing out an ill archer or one with a sprained ankle, etc. It pays to be prepared.

II

BOWHUNTING

5

Bowhunting Equipment

HUNTING BOWS

Bows made from laminations of wood and fiberglass or molded from strands of fiberglass are now the choice of almost every bowhunter. The development of fiberglass literally revolutionized the manufacture of bows, initiating mass-production techniques. Previous to that time, hunting bows had been made of wood. Osage orange and yew bows were in the elite class; lemonwood and hickory bows in the economy class. Wood bows are less efficient than laminated wood and fiberglass or solid fiberglass bows. However, a properly handmade osage orange or yew bow is still an effective weapon as well as a lot of fun to fashion. Lemonwood and hickory bows are still marketed for novices, but they are not recommended for hunting.

Most efficient modern-day hunting bows will cast a 1-ounce hunting arrow at speeds of slightly above 200 feet per second. This represents roughly 39 foot-pounds of striking power, enough to drive a sharp broadhead completely through a deer.

Selecting the proper hunting bow to fit the person involved requires experience or a knowledge of requirements. A bow should be no stronger than the archer can handle without strain and shoot with accuracy. However, some degree of compromise may be necessary as one must also consider the laws of the state involved and the species to be hunted. One must first know if the state in which he intends to hunt has a minimum bow-weight requirement. For big-game hunting, several states require a minimum pull of 40 lbs. Since the pull strength varies with the length of the draw (effective length of arrow), each archer must make certain his bow has 40 lbs. of pull at his length of draw. One state requires a minimum pull of 30 lbs.; some avoid reference to pull and require a bow that can cast the archer's hunting arrow 150 yards. A few states, including Michigan, have no minimum weight or distance of cast requirement for hunting bows. Experience in that state has indicated that there is little need for laws stipulating a minimum pull for bows used for deer hunting. Hunters naturally select bows with adequate pull because of reasons of pride.

Bow and arrow hunters usually use as heavy a bow as they can handle, which for most men is between 40 and 60 lbs. A few use bows too heavy and thereby sacrifice a degree of accuracy. Most women cannot be expected to shoot a hunting bow with more than 30 to 35 lbs. pull at their length of arrow. For this reason, states with a 40-lb. minimum pull are in effect discouraging women from participating in the grand sport of bow and arrow deer hunting.

If the game hunted is elk, bear, or wild hogs, a bow with a pull of at least 50 lbs. is recommended.

Whether you select a straight model, one with a short stiff recurve, or one with a long working recurve is a matter of personal preference and how much emphasis is put on smoothness of performance (Fig. 5–1). Each of the types is quite adequate for hunting. Generally, bows of about 5 feet in length are preferred for hunting because they are easier to handle in brushy areas.

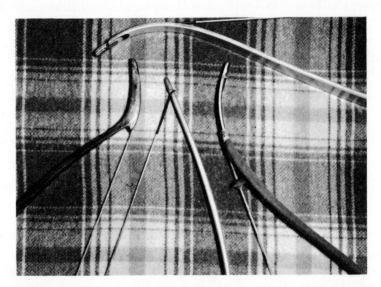

Fig. 5–1. The tip of a bow may provide a clue to its type: (*top*) the working recurve end of a modern field bow, (*left*) tip of an osage orange wood hunting bow with built-in bush nock, (*center*) straight-ended target bow, (*right*) working recurve-tipped hunting bow with rubber "brush buttons" to keep brush and weeds from lodging in the angle between the string and bow. The limb of this last bow is covered with olive-drab material for camouflage purposes.

Crossbows are regarded as illegal for bowhunting in most states. Bowhunters and field archers themselves had a hand in getting the crossbow outlawed in special bowhunting seasons. Their reason for this stand was to discourage and/or exclude from bowhunting individuals who did not have the full interest of bowhunting at heart. It was believed violators might be more apt to be attracted to bowhunting seasons if they could use a crossbow, which requires little archery skill. Died-in-the-wool archers did not want any regulations that might invite violators or poor sportsmen into the ranks of bowhunters who were still fighting to secure separate and/or to expand existing bowhunting seasons. Poor sportsmanship and violations, then as well as now, are detrimental to our grand sport.

HUNTING ARROWS

Hunting arrow materials now include wood, glass, forgewood (wood that has been urea impregnated and compressed), and aluminum. In the earlier days of bow and arrow deer hunting in America, Port Orford cedar, Norway pine, Douglas fir, and birch shafts were the prime materials out of which arrows were made. However, Port Orford cedar, the older time-tested arrow material, still leads the market for shafts (see Fig. 5–4). The use of glass is increasing year by year.

Port Orford shafts are the most economical. Glass, forgewood, and aluminum arrows, although more expensive, are preferred by many archers because they stay straight. The extra weight of forgewood makes them a favorite of many who seek maximum penetration on the larger game species such as boar, elk, moose, and bear. In general, hunting arrows ought to weigh an ounce or slightly more (437 to 525 grains).

In purchasing arrows, be absolutely certain that they have the correct spine (stiffness) to shoot properly in your bow. Know the weight of your bow and demand appropriately spined arrows. Check the manufacturer's recommendations stamped on the arrow box to make certain that they are meant for your bow weight. Also check to see whether or not the shafts are straight. If they are crooked, do not buy them as they will not fly straight.

In the interest of safety to yourself, be certain that the broadhead arrows are of proper length or slightly longer than necessary so as to avoid over-drawing. The length of a broadhead is measured from the base of the head, which should come to rest against your index finger at full draw if the head is set vertically. If it is set horizontally on the shaft, it will come to rest against the back of the bow at full draw. For these reasons, broadhead arrows will usually be from ½ to 1½ inches longer than target arrows. For information on how to measure the length of arrows, see page 176.

When it comes to selecting a broadhead for your big-game arrows, there is an abundance of shapes to select from (Fig. 5–2 and 5–3). In general, most heads can be classified as single blade (two cutting edges), three bladed (bodkin, three cutting edges), and four bladed (four cutting edges), and some with modifications of the above. Manufacturers claim many attributes for their own patented brands of heads. Any of the types mentioned are adequate if set perfectly straight on a straight shaft so that it will fly as straight as it is shot. When and if an arrow dives off course after flying

Fig. 5–2. A sample of some of the many types of arrowheads available following World War II. Nos. 1, 3, and 4 are used in field archery. No. 2 is used for roving and for small-game hunting. No. 5 is an Indian arrowhead included for comparison. Nos. 6–8 represent single-bladed, four-bladed, and three-bladed arrowheads used for big game. A barbed fishing point is illustrated by No. 9.

Fig. 5–3. Most of the broadheads in use during the early 1940's were crude in comparison to later types. Most heads at that time had parallel holes for fitting them onto the arrow shaft.

25 to 30 yards or more, it is not the arrowhead you should blame; the fault is likely a result of a crooked shaft, a poorly set head, or feathers that are too small for the size of the broadhead.

Arrows with more than two cutting edges ought to be used whenever possible. The extra cutting by the extra blades adds to the chances of cutting more arteries and therefore may cut down on the distance a deer will run, thereby making your task of retrieving an easier one.

There is some merit in the argument that single-bladed and four-bladed arrows on which the cross-blade is made of thin razor steel are superior for penetration when a bone such as the shoulder blade is hit. It is believed that the thin cross-blade will break or collapse if it encounters bone, thereby permitting deeper penetration by the main blade. Regardless of the type of arrowhead used, it should be sharpened by filing before it is used to shoot deer or other big game. Most heads are dull-edged when marketed.

Another point to make certain of is that the broadhead you use in hunting is of legal size. Some states stipulate that broadheads used for deer hunting must be at least a certain size or larger. Others only go so far as to require that broadhead arrows must be used. Some stipulate a minimum width of ¾ inch for heads. Heads with a width of ⅞ to 1 inch are preferred by most hunters. The width of the three-bladed arrows cannot be measured in the usual way. Their effective size is usually determined by the diameter of the hole that they will just barely pass through.

Broadhead arrows used for big game should all be fletched with feathers set on a slight spiral so as to give the arrows a spin as they fly (Fig. 5–4). This spin has a tendency to keep the arrow, even if slightly crooked, turning and driving toward the mark in a small corkscrew-like pattern. It reduces chances of an arrow darting off course.

Arrows with blunt heads are most commonly used for small game such as squirrels and cottontails. Such an arrow delivers greater shock. Then too, if it misses a squirrel, it will glance off the limb instead of sticking in the treetop.

Arrows for squirrels commonly are fletched with a long feather wrapped spirally around the nock end and are called flu flus. The spirally wrapped feather offers great wind resistance, causing the arrow to drop back to earth, probably no more than 35 yards away, even when shot at a squirrel overhead. A similar braking effect, although less effective, is provided by setting four feathers and leaving them untrimmed. At 20 yards or less, these arrows strike almost as hard as a conventionally fletched arrow. Broadheads used for hunting pheasants should be flu flu fletched. It is a matter of common sense and safety as well as economy that arrows shot at flying game birds and game mammals in trees should be fletched so as to bring them back to earth at a slow and safe rate of fall if the arrow misses. Then too such arrows are easier to find as they usually hit and stand almost straight up in the ground.

Fig. 5–4. Broadheads used for big-game hunting should be fletched with conventional-shaped feathers as shown at the bottom. The top two arrows represent two of several modifications of flu flu–type fletching commonly employed on blunt arrows and broadheads used for squirrel and game-bird hunting. The shafts are of Port Orford cedar.

HUNTING QUIVERS

Three types of quivers are most commonly used in bow and arrow hunting. They are the shoulder quiver, the middle-of-the-back quiver, and the bow quiver.

Shoulder quivers are most popular for carrying hunting arrows. There are several reasons for their general acceptance. They are large enough for carrying about a dozen arrows. A dividing strap makes it possible to separate blunt and/or field arrows from the broadheads. When properly adjusted, the quiver hangs so that the nock end of the arrows are at a most convenient place for quick availability of additional arrows (Figs. 4–1 and 6–9). The better models have a special zippered pocket for carrying necessary accessories such as the hunting license, the special deer tag (seal), an extra bowstring, first aid kit, a 6-inch file, a small pocket hone, and perhaps a hunting knife if you do not carry a sheath knife on your belt.

Middle-of-the-back quivers are most commonly used in brushy hunting areas. They are a great asset in the bush country. This quiver is long enough to extend up past the feathers to the nock end of the arrows. This feature protects the feathers from getting messed up by brush encountered by the stalking archer. Since the top of the quiver is immediately behind the neck of the archer, it is still readily accessible (see Figs. 6–6 and 9–3). Snow and rain may be kept from the arrows and feathers by means of a plastic cover. An elastic-edged plastic refrigerator cover of the type used by housewives to cover small bowls serves nicely for covering the top of the quiver. Some of these quivers have individual leather arrowhead pockets in their bottom for keeping the sharpened broadheads separate. A ring of bristles has been placed at a position just below the feathers in some models of quivers. The bristles keep the shafts from rattling by keeping them apart.

The bow quiver is an innovation that made its appearance in the early 1940's. It consists of a special bracket that fastens to the bow near the handle section and holds three or four arrows in a ready position slightly to one side of the handle (see Fig. A–3). These quivers do not interfere with the clear view needed for shooting, nor with the movement of the arrow or string on releasing the shaft. The principal advantage of the bow quiver is its extreme handiness and the fact that the arrows are held separately so that the heads will stay sharp. Some quivers are held on by means of a screw; others can be temporarily taped on. Another asset of the bow quiver is that in placing a second or third arrow on the string, a minimum of movement is required, thereby lessening the chance of betraying the archer's location to the animal hunted.

A type of hip quiver has recently appeared on the market, but it has not yet been on the market long enough to indicate its acceptance by bowhunters. The old-fashioned target-type belt quiver that hangs alongside the archer's thigh is seldom used by modern-day hunting archers.

ACCESSORY EQUIPMENT

Accessory equipment for the bowhunter includes a suitable armguard and a shooting glove or fingertab.

Since cold weather during most big-game bow and arrow seasons requires warm clothing, bulkiness of clothing on the bow arm may interfere with free passage of the bowstring. For this reason, an armguard large enough to keep the loose clothing from interfering with the string is essential. This often necessitates an armguard that is slightly larger than the one usually used in field archery. Beginning bowhunters are most apt to have trouble in this respect.

Many archers prefer a shooting glove for hunting because it offers excellent protection to the fingers that draw the string. An additional advantage is that it permits a rapid grasping of the string for a quick shot.

Fingertabs, though they cause a quick shot at a fleeing deer to be somewhat slower, provide a smoother release for many archers and thereby facilitate accuracy in shooting.

6

How To Hunt Your Deer

Deer hunting is one of the oldest and one of the most enjoyable and challenging outdoors sports available. The reward in the hunt, whether you bag a deer or not, is considerable. Trying to outwit this crafty game animal offers a real challenge. Here a sportsman has a chance to pit his skill and knowledge against one of nature's smartest animals. Imagine, if you will, man who lives and works in a city an average of 50 weeks each year coming into the forest to try to outsmart a deer in its own backyard.

Deer know every foot of their home area and are smart enough not to let themselves be chased into strange surroundings. Follow one on fresh snow sometime and you will see how it turns, backtracks, and circles, but refuses to leave its home area. Of course there are rare exceptions, as there are in almost anything.

Deer owe their lives to the fact that they have outsmarted their enemies day in and day out. Those that did not are no longer alive to be hunted. It is a case of survival of the fittest. After all, the old doe from the beginning teaches her young that survival depends on remaining unseen and unheard. Life for a deer is a game of hide-and-seek, with the death penalty for mistakes. Imagine the experience in survival tactics an old buck must have had.

These facts make it obvious that when an archer goes deer hunting, he is competing against one of nature's champions. Is it any wonder, then, that many hunters fail to see deer in the forest?

It is probably a fair guess that at least ten deer see a hunter for every deer that the hunter may glimpse. Maybe the ratio is even more one-sided. Woods sense is necessary for the deer's survival. Perhaps a good motto for the average bowhunter would be to stop, look, and listen to see if the distant shadows are hiding an "educated" deer.

During the rutting season, some bucks grow bold when overcome with mating desire. Increased mortality of bucks hit by cars during the rut each fall results from such increased boldness and loss of their usual good sense of caution.

The killing of moose on railroad tracks in Alaska likewise increases during the rut. Old bulls become so antagonistic that they refuse to yield ground even to locomotives.

In order to get the most sport out of deer hunting, one must know about their daily habits. Such knowledge gives the hunter a sporting chance to outsmart them. It takes heartbreaking experience as well as diligent study to gain the knowledge needed to properly check an area for deer signs and not to bobble any opportunities for a shot. Such checking, however, is necessary before you can properly plan your hunting strategy. Should you hunt the area from a blind along a runway, stalk, or depend on a drive of some sort? Maybe a combination of the methods is desirable? Since the fun is in the hunt, you will want to select the method that will give you the most satisfaction.

SCOUTING THE HUNTING AREA

A bowhunter should, if possible, scout his prospective hunting area a week or two before the season opens. It is of limited value, however, to scout territory a month or more before the season. This is true because in late summer deer are still scattered on their summer range. When the first frosts occur, deer frequently shift their area of movement; and "buck signs" show up. The mating prowl is on or will start soon. In mountain country, the area in which the deer are active will depend on snows to drive them to lower altitudes or to initiate their migration.

When you first scout a prospective hunting area in the lake or prairie states, drive around a bit after a rain or snow to check for fresh tracks along country or woods roads (Fig. 6–1). Deer trails may or may not be visible

Fig. 6–1. Tracks of deer tell a story if you can read them. This deer was moving in the direction pointed by the shotgun shell. Soft ground allowed the cloven hoofs of this medium-sized deer to spread and the dew claws to mark the ground. A very heavy deer taking long strides on hard ground may show similar but larger footprints. There is no sure way to tell a buck track from a doe track.

from the road. Deer often travel a trail in the thick woods and then fan out over a 15- to 20-yard wide area where they cross a road. Just because you find no tracks crossing the roads, do not give up. Maybe another hunter beat you to the track and resorted to an old trick used on many an occasion. Several years back, other hunters frequently converged on the area where one of the authors hunted. Apparently they thought that because he lived on the area, any site he hunted must be good. They got fooled in more ways than one. To decrease competition at favorite hunting sites, he used to take a small tree branch and brush out all fresh tracks on trails in the vicinity. This did two things: it discouraged competition and provided a chance to see when fresh signs appeared. The result may have been disheartening to the novices who spent most of their time road hunting and therefore could not find any "signs." Experienced bowmen, however, prowled the woods looking for other types of signs, signs that could not be erased. They had developed real deer sense.

Both eternal hopes and the blood pressure of a hunter rise when he locates signs of buck activity. Look for brush or saplings from which the bark has been scraped at a height of between 1 and 3 feet above the ground (Fig. 7–2). Saplings up to about 3 inches in diameter are commonly used for rubbing the velvet off the antlers, or are "horned" instinctively during the rut. In some cases, trees up to about 6 inches in diameter may be scraped. Where they occur, ash, maple, aspen, willows, or spruces seem to suffer considerable "barking." Areas pawed or scraped clean of leaves may indicate signs of recent use by bucks. These frequently occur as widened spots at intervals in trails. Fresh droppings can be identified by their shiny surface and softness when pinched between the fingers. Experience will teach you roughly how old a track is by its degree of shininess. Perhaps, if you are a non-smoker, you may even smell a "rank" deer as you steal silently through the woods. There may be old deer "beds" in certain areas and signs of deer traveling from bedding areas to a stand of oaks with a good acorn crop or to alfalfa or cornfields.

Another advantage to scouting the area ahead of time is that it minimizes chances of becoming lost in the excitement of stalking or trailing a deer.

If you have done a good job of inventorying for signs, and have learned the lay of the land, you are now ready to settle down to hunting in earnest.

Deer ordinarily feed and travel most during twilight hours, before sunrise and after sunset. During the dark of the moon and at times when it is clouded over all night, deer activity is even greater during twilight periods. Where the hours of legal hunting permit, the hunter should plan to be in the woods before daylight, and in the evening he should plan to stay until dark. Since morning activity dwindles by mid-morning and then increases again from about 3:00 P.M. until dark, the hunter will do well to stay out until at least 9:30 A.M. and to resume hunting again about 3:00 P.M.

Where a lot of hunters stir around in the area at all hours of the day, or when the rut is in progress, chances for a shot at a deer are good at any time of the day. Most hunters, however, relax during the mid-day hours, comparing notes about their morning hunts and shooting at marks to improve their marksmanship (Fig. 6–2).

Fig. 6–2. A little clowning and practice during mid-day when the deer usually lie quiet can add many fond memories to the hunt.

HUNTING FROM A BLIND

When deer use a runway regularly, or when they daily drift from a definite bedding ground to a feeding area, hunting from a blind or a well-selected stand between bedding and feeding areas may be rewarding. This is the technique most commonly used by Michigan bowhunters in years past. Hunters in such areas commonly select a suitable site for the blind at a spot about 20 yards downwind from the trail. With the wind blowing from the trail toward the blind, any deer traveling on the trail will be unable to scent the hunter. Where possible, the blind should be established in or next to natural cover where the background of trees or brush will break up the silhouette of the hunter and his blind (Figs. 6–3 and 6–4).

When you make your blind, cut the needed branches from trees or brush away from the immediate site. Bring the brush to the site of the blind and stick the butt ends of the branches into the ground, setting them in a cir-

Fig. 6–3. Selecting a proper background for a deer hunting blind is important. Brushy background to hide the silhouette of the hunter is just as important as is the front of the blind, which helps conceal the hunter's movements.

Fig. 6–4. Camouflage clothing and equipment and this good natural blind contributed to the taking of a white-tailed deer from this spot. Note the value of using the bow limb to screen and hide part of the bowhunter's face. (Photograph by D. Hoopes.)

cular arrangement so that the blind will have an open central area at least 6 feet across. Make the walls of brush just dense enough to permit careful movement on the inside, without being seen from the trail, and just high enough to permit concealment while sitting in comfort on a stump, stone, log, or stool. Only the top of your head should be visible from the outside. Two or three "shooting windows" through a jagged top edge of the blind will facilitate shooting. The brush for making the blind should match other cover in the area to keep it inconspicuous. When possible, it is well to construct the blind a day or two ahead of its use. All leaves should be raked from the ground inside the structure to permit movement of the feet without noise. In such a blind, you can sit quietly by the hour and expectantly wait for your deer to come. If the wind is unfavorable for use of the blind (blowing from the blind toward the trail) on a particular day, do not use it that day.

While occupying the blind, a hunter should direct full attention toward detecting or locating the deer while it is still a long way off. This is no time to doze or relax.

Listen intently for sounds and look *into* the surrounding cover for signs of a moving leg or the flicking of an ear or tail. Use field glasses if you have a pair. They will add effectiveness and fun to your hunt. Whether you smoke or not will not make much difference so far as smell is concerned, because if the wind is such that the deer can smell the smoke, you may be sure it also can scent you. The worst giveaway so far as smoking is concerned is the incessant nervous movements of the smoker. Habits of cigarette-smoking deer hunters have been observed on several occasions. Their white ungloved hands kept flashing up and down to and from their face almost constantly. Any half-awake deer within a quarter-mile could have seen these hand-waving hunters. They may as well have shouted "yo-hoo" at the same time. It is no wonder some hunters do not get a deer near their blind. Hunters will have to learn to control or deny such craving as smoking during the best hunting hours of the day. Flashing your face from side to side for quick glimpses of the area is equally disturbing.

When you can sit so still that a squirrel enters your blind, a ruffed grouse walks up to you, and a songbird perches on your arrow, then you have developed the ability to become a good blind-hunter. It is a frame of mind. You can sit that still if you make up your mind to. Others have done it for years.

There is a time to move as well as a time not to. The decision to do either is yours. Do you have the self-control and ability to "pull the wool over the deer's eyes"? Or will you be a blundering hunter in the eyes of the many deer that may spot and skillfully avoid you?

Some states permit the use of trees or elevated perches for deer hunting; others declare off-the-ground shooting stands illegal. Before you use this method for hunting deer, be sure to check on its legality in your state.

Elevated shooting positions may be selected on suitably located large limbs of trees or be prepared from poles or lumber (Fig. 6–5). Special seats can even be purchased for fastening to tree trunks. A word of caution regarding hunting from such elevated perches in the gun season seems in order. People in trees have been mistaken and shot for bear in sections where this game animal is found. Such mistakes may never occur in a bow and arrow season, but it seems wise not to invite trouble if you hunt in the regular season.

Fig. 6–5. A tree blind provides an excellent view of the surrounding habitat. A hunter's movements and scent are more difficult for a deer to detect in such a position. Tree blinds are illegal in some states. (Photograph by D. Hoopes.)

If you decide to use a tree blind, do considerable practicing from such a position before you settle down to hunt in earnest. It is a strange and difficult position from which to shoot accurately. In parts of the South-eastern states, where ground cover is dense, hunting from elevated blinds is just about the only way a hunter can get a clear view of his quarry. The elevated position has an added advantage in that it makes it difficult for deer to detect the hunter's scent.

Cold is probably the biggest handicap to blind-hunting. You have to wear almost twice as much clothing as you expect to need and ought to have a pocket hand-warmer to light and drop down your back. This will do wonders to keep you comfortable and still.

STALKING IS FUN

If it is fun and a real challenge you are after, try stalking your deer. However, it will take a lot of "deer sense" and extraordinary patience if you are to be rewarded with meat as well as fun from your hunt. You will have to become adept at being quiet and at using cover to screen or conceal movement. Deer are endowed with three exceptionally keen senses that keep them out of the clutches of their enemies; namely, hearing, sight, and the sense of smell.

The large ears of deer serve as efficient sound catchers. They can be moved freely and independently to pinpoint the source of sounds.

A new-born fawn under observation a few years ago showed early instinctive use of two instincts. Within 8 minutes after birth, a 7-lb. buck fawn had found the doe's nipple and nursed contentedly. When only 28 minutes old, it perked up and cupped its ears at the sound of a car driving by on a street about 75 yards away. Other fawns were seen to similarly locate sounds when only 46 and 75 minutes old. It is remarkable how they not only heard the sound so soon but also cupped their ears properly to spot the direction from which it came.

Deer seem especially adept at detecting movement. They are not so keen at identifying stationary objects, however. This is suggestive of color blindness, which at times seems compensated for by the ability to spot anything that moves. As in the case with other wild ruminants, they tend to feed mostly during twilight. The presence of natural enemies tends to accentuate feeding at these hours and decreases activity during the daytime. The presence of a four-compartment stomach also seems adapted to such short-period hurried feeding. In other words, deer have the "equipment" that normally is present in animals that feed during the short dawn and dusk periods.

Animals that are active at night or under semidark conditions are ordinarily color blind. Apparently color vision is of little or no use under such poor-light conditions; and since it has no survival value, it did not develop. Cats, and monkeys that are active mostly at night, are color blind. Species of monkeys that are up and about in the daytime, like man, have well-developed color vision.

There is no experimental evidence to indicate whether or not deer have any degree of color vision; but circumstantial evidence indicates that they probably see things only in shades of gray, as one sees a black and white photograph. This viewpoint is concurred in by some prominent medical authorities.

The quality and type of eyesight of deer make it important that a hunter, if he is to move about at all, should use clothing that when viewed without the benefit of color should appear drab and of intermediate shades that come reasonably close to matching the pattern and shading of surrounding cover patterns. Proper use of mixed shades such as occurs in camouflage clothing will "break up" the outline of the hunter's appearance and reduce chances of having his movement detected. Nature on a breezy day is constantly moving: leaves waving and/or falling, and bushes swaying. All this adds to the difficulties for a deer trying to spot movement where the hunter's outline is broken up.

Man's usual rhythmic movement may be a giveaway. He goes through the woods with a crunch, crunch, crunch at each foot-fall. Such regular timing is out of step with noises made by wild creatures. Man further goes heel and toe, heel and toe, with a prolonged crun-n-n-nch, which indeed is a foreign sound in the woods. Because the feet of wild beasts are small, they produce a shorter and sharper noise with frequent interruptions. It is also believed that the legs of the hunter as they flash past each other produce the effect of a sort of heliograph to advertise his presence. Watch a hunter go by in the woods some time and you will notice how his legs flash, flash, flash signals to the side as he trudges by. Proper camouflage trousers will help cover some leg movement; however, they are not a complete substitute for special care in stalking habits. It is obvious that if a hunter uses tennis shoes in his stalking, he should select a pair of olive drab color, or daub them with brown shoe polish. White shoes are to be avoided like poison.

The deer's sense of smell is second to none. Let a deer get a whiff of you and it will dash or sneak away. A deer may take a second look and may even listen twice to make sure, but there will be no second guessing once it gets your scent. For this reason, it is absolutely necessary that you at least walk diagonally into the wind while stalking. When hunting along slopes of mountains, remember that your scent will drift upslope when the temperatures are rising during the day and will drift downslope as the evening shadows lengthen and the atmosphere starts cooling off.

Stalking consists of finding a deer by stealth, and then approaching it to the point of delivering a successful arrow—all this so carefully executed that the deer is outwitted. It is well to repeat at this point that you must move silently as a cat, minimize movement by going very slowly and intermittently, that you must use cover as a screen when available, and that you work toward the wind.

When sleuthing in an area and trying to catch sight of a deer for closer stalking, it is well to move no faster than a mile an hour. This slow approach when regularly interrupted with sit a little, stand a little, and hesitate a little, between *toe* and *heel* steps, may allow you to spot a deer before it sees you. This is an important point of advantage. See it first and do not get caught at it (Fig. 6-6).

Fig. 6–6. Still-hunting in the land of the Spanish moss on Alabama's Tombigbee River is a most pleasant way to hunt. Sneaking and/or standing along such trails at dawn and dusk may be rewarding. Deer trails crossing such roads should receive special attention.

Remember to look for a moving foot, ear, tail, or the outline of some part of the body not screened by vegetation. A small pair of field glasses is useful for examining distant patches of cover for partially hidden deer. If you suddenly see a whole deer at close quarters, it will be a mighty "rut-happy" buck or a very stupid deer. Such a sudden appearance is a sign that you did not do a good job of looking when the animal was still partly screened by cover. It is a sign that you made a mistake; but because you made it while standing or sitting quietly, luck still came your way.

Where possible, take advantage of cover by advancing with a screen of trees or bushes ahead as you stalk. If there is a slight dip in the ground, or an old ditch present, use it to screen foot movement. Where possible, keep only your head in view above cover. When you approach the crest of a hill, approach it only to the point where you can stop and peer over the brow with only your head showing. Ease ahead step by step and carefully examine more of the hidden area on the far side. When moving parallel with the hill, stay to one side of the crest and peer over the ridge at intervals to carefully examine the upwind side.

If it is a ravine or an arroyo you are approaching, peer into it by peeking over the edge; then withdraw and stealthily move ahead and peer into it again and again at intervals. The same tactic is equally suited for hunting areas below a shelf of rock on which the hunter is stalking.

If some distant noise such as from a car or a passing train occurs, use the disturbance to screen your own movement. At such a time, there will be no need to worry about making minor noises as they will not be heard anyway.

A cover of snow may be used to your advantage. Tracking conditions make it possible to find where deer are active and makes it easier to spot them. Conversely, it also makes it easier for deer to see the moving feet of the hunter. A blanket of snow also simplifies tracking and recovery of your animal when you score a successful hit. Do not be discouraged if you do not find many fresh tracks on the morning following the season's first snow. On occasions in the Allegan Forest in Michigan, deer seemed to lie in their beds for a whole day following the first snow, if it came while they were bedded down. After all, the presence of snow was a new condition for all the fawns in the herd.

One time a big buck disappeared in a stand of bushes. In an attempt to relocate the animal, the hunter dropped to his hands and knees and peered under the second-growth oak brush. Movement of two deer's legs was noticed about 150 yards upwind. Their movement was watched just long enough to determine what they were doing. The hunter then withdrew and circled to a better spot for stalking. From a closer view, the deer were seen feeding on acorns. When they put their noses to the ground to feed, their eyes disappeared below the snow line.

Using good "cat tactics," the hunter moved only a step or two each time the deer dipped their heads below the snow line to feed on acorns exposed by pawing. He eventually worked his way to within about 20 yards, but brush screened any possibility for a shot. One deer finally became suspicious. (Dressed in dark-colored clothing, the hunter must have "stood out" like a sore thumb, standing there on the white blanket of snow.) The buck started to circle to test the wind for suspicious scent. Moving slowly, very slowly, and continuously, the hunter drew his bow in the direction of an opening in the brush behind which the buck was moving. At 16 yards the arrow flashed forward and carved its way completely through the deer. The buck collapsed while on the "dead" run just 70 yards from where shot. The archer's first deer was in the bag.

On another occasion, a large buck was spotted half a mile distant. It was in an open abandoned field with rolling ground. The cover consisted of hip-high grasses and weeds. From his hilltop vantage point, the hunter watched until the buck's direction of movement was determined. Then the hunter "slipped" from the knoll and ran toward a spot the buck would surely pass if it continued its direction of movement. Within about 25 yards of the spot, the hunter spotted a pair of antlers and the top of the buck's head "peeking" over the top of the knoll directly above. Tall grass and camouflage from head to foot helped hide the archer. The buck, however, must have heard or seen movement as it immediately withdrew to circle toward the very point the hunter had been trying to get to in the first place. As soon as its antlers disappeared, the bowhunter dashed on toward the spot the animal would certainly have to pass; but the dry grass underfoot seemed noisier than ever. Again a pair of antlers peered over a rise in the ground, but the buck still seemed suspicious and again hesitated even though the wind prevented him from scenting the archer. Once more the animal withdrew behind the knoll and started to circle in the opposite direction. There was no doubt now what it was up to; it hoped to circle downwind and around the suspicious spot in an attempt to scent the source of danger. The archer turned and dashed downwind (wind blowing on his back) and around the brow of the hill. There was no time to avoid making noise now. Speed seemed most important of all.

The archer got there first and was crouched and waiting as the buck topped the rise. As it came into view, it turned sideways. Out of the grass arose the hunter while simultaneously drawing the bow and releasing the arrow—all in one continuous movement. The last move in that "checker game" was the bowhunter's. A trophy buck weighing 237 lbs. on the hoof was in the bag (Fig. 6–7). Tall grass and rolling ground for cover and a steady wind had made a successful stalk possible. Camouflage clothing had helped hide the hunter and had confused the buck in the "sneak" approach.

Wherever cover is lacking or very short, you may well have to finish your stalk by crawling flat on the ground. Anyone who has been in the infantry knows the value of staying close to the ground and sticking to the tiniest depressions to remain hidden. If you have to move where cover is scarce, do so only when the deer's head is down to the ground. For some reason, a deer does not seem to notice movement so quickly while its head is in that position. A deer's head is usually not at ground level very long at a time, and if you try to move too many steps at one time you will surely get caught in the act. To keep from getting discovered, remember that a feeding deer usually wags its tail from side to side just before it raises its head. Stop dead still as soon as the tail wags, as the head will be raised almost immediately. Time your deer and you may be able to figure out about how many steps you can safely take each time it lowers its head.

When the opportunity for your shot comes, draw your bow very slowly and shoot in one continuous movement. By using such slow-draw tactics, deer have been shot while they looked directly at the archer. On the other hand, a quick snap-shot once was tried at a deer that unexpectedly crowded one of the authors to within 5 yards. The string had not been drawn back 6 inches before the deer was many yards away and in thick cover. The lesson from that episode was that you cannot outdraw a deer; you just have

Fig. 6–7. A 237-lb. (live weight) Iowa whitetail buck stalked by A. O. Haugen. (Photograph by Floyd Thomas.)

to do your quick-draw shooting without getting caught at it. To a deer, anything that moves fast is a possible source of danger.

The speed of deer is exemplified by an occasion where one at 17 yards jumped at the sound of the "twang" of the string and had whirled 90 degrees by the time the arrow got there. If the arrow speed out of that 55-lb. yew bow was 160 feet per second, it meant that in $\frac{1}{3}$ second, the deer had evaded a broadside hit. Other hunters have reported similar disheartening misses as a result of quick movement by deer. Such immediate response is probably the result of the deer suspecting danger and being especially alert and ready to react.

DRIVE HUNTING

When the usual morning peak of activity has died down, and the animals have gone to their bedding grounds to spend the day chewing their cud and watching for enemies, a properly organized drive may produce some excitement and shooting. There are several modifications of drives, depending on the lay of the land and distribution of food and cover. If the area to be driven is an arroyo or narrow streambed with cover, one or more standers should go by a circuitous route to the head end where they select shooting stands in suitable cover. If there are one or more sidedraws to the ravine, other standers may take positions there. Then one or two drivers may slowly stalk up through the cover of the main ravine to move any deer present past one or more of the standers. The drivers have just as good a chance of getting a shot as do the standers. This is true because even where drivers make considerable noise on purpose, at least a third of the animals circle and make their way back through the driving line rather than allow themselves to be forceably driven like cattle. Deer are extremely contrary animals and usually do the opposite of what you try to force them to do. This habit, when known, may be used to the hunter's advantage.

This contrariness of deer is best exemplified by a doe once used in experiments. Helpers had been instructed to crate and weigh the animal. The crating process consisted of using a sheet of plywood to force her to the wall in a corner of her pen and then putting a crate at one end of the plywood and allowing her to escape the confinement by entering the crate. She would go to the crate entrance, but there she stopped and refused to budge even when forceably pushed. However, when one of the handlers finally reached over the plywood sheet, grabbed her by the tail, and pulled away from the crate, she walked on in, having her tail stretched as she did so. Stubborn? Yes, or is it a trait of being contrary?

In rough country such as occurs in mountains, hunters oft'times walk parallel to each other along the slopes. Where saddles or lower elevation crossovers occur at the head of side canyons or draws, the hunter on the upper side stays a little ahead so that he will get to such natural crossover areas in time to intercept deer jumped by the hunters at lower elevations. Where all hunters walk parallel along the slopes well below crossover saddles, or on long wooded mountain ridges in the East, the upper hunters may lag behind the hunters below so as to intercept any deer that tries to circle above and sneak behind the hunter that jumped it. This up-hill circling habit of deer is common.

At times hunters on flat ground may cautiously move ahead abreast in a line at 100-yard intervals with a second line of hunters coming along behind the first after about a 5-minute delay. The strategy is to move deer so that the deer may be seen by the hunters to the side or behind as the animal tries to elude the person who disturbed it. This type of driving amounts to a sort of organized still-hunt—alternately sneaking, standing, sneaking some more, and then maybe even walking boldly for 50 yards, etc.

Even where driven by dogs, such as is commonly done in the Southeast, deer do not necessarily panic when "pushed" toward the line of shooters. Deer being chased by dogs often jump aside into a thicket and let the baying hounds and yapping mongrels go by on the track of another deer. Other deer have been noted to run upwind to and then parallel to the line of standers until they smelled an opening in the "wall" of hunters and then dashed through to safety. It is no wonder deer have survived and still thrive in the face of intense land use and increasing human pressures.

An important point to remember in any hunting technique is to be flexible enough to modify your style to fit the situation. Your hunting tactics may be influenced by any one or more of the following: the lay of the land, wind conditions, dampness or dryness of the ground cover (silent or noisy walking conditions), the progress of the rut, the time of day, manpower, and personal inclinations.

Study your situation and then plan and execute your hunt with the greatest of care. After the hunt is over, go back over your results and note well your mistakes or good fortune. If you keep a diary of your hunts, you will add more fun to your future hunts.

AIM TO RETRIEVE

A deer when it suddenly appears before an expectant archer seemingly comes out of nowhere. As a result of the sudden excitement that follows, the critter may look as big as a horse; or so it seems anyway. The excited archer frequently forgets to pick a spot at which to aim and shoots at the general silhouette, scoring a poor hit or missing altogether.

For consistency and better shooting, it is important that the hunter carefully select a vital spot on the deer and concentrate on it as the one and only spot to hit. Not just any spot will do because some areas are more vital than others. Since arrows kill by hemorrhage, it is important that they strike where blood vessels are numerous. The general area with such a condition is the rib section, the back edge of which houses the liver, and the front three-fourths of which houses the heart and lungs.

On the average, the chest section of an adult whitetail measures about 9 inches top to bottom and 15 inches front to back. The top to bottom measurement includes the backbone but excludes the bony processes that project upward from the backbone. The inner cavity with vital organs is only about 6 inches high. In other words, if you exclude the neck and backbone, you have to place your arrow in an area about the size of two 6-inch targets placed side by side for best success. You may be inclined to think the authors are in error. They are not. The measurements were made from the cleaned rib cage of a yearling doe (Fig. 6–8).

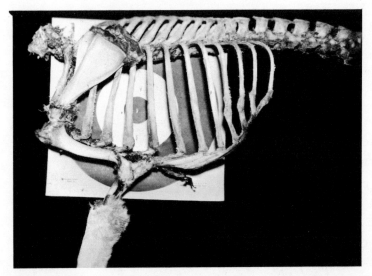

Fig. 6–8. The primary killing area on a deer is indicated by the 12-inch field archery face placed inside the rib cage of this yearling doe whitetail. The white 5-ring indicates the size of the main killing area as being only about 6 inches top to bottom and 14 inches front to back. Hunters should concentrate on the "black spot" area for best results.

It is generally best to aim for the area of the heart, which lies in the bottom of the chest cavity just above where the front leg joins the chest (Fig. 6–9). On the exterior of the body, this spot is located about one-third of the way up on the chest and above the front leg. Do not aim behind the leg; a hit there will miss the heart.

The upper leg bone (humerus) and the shoulder blade offer no serious obstacle as they do not overlie the heart. If you hit the upper front leg bone, your shot was too low for a killing shot. A hit in the shoulder blade likewise would be a poor hit even if it is penetrated by an arrow from a strong bow.

There are at least three good reasons for aiming at a spot only a third of the way up on the chest. The first is that it centers on the heart area. Second, a deer may "squat" down slightly in preparation for its takeoff jump as soon as it hears the twang of the bowstring. The below-center spot leaves a slight reserve area that can be hit if such happens. A high hit in the chest will still pierce the lungs. Third, archers seem to have a natural tendency to miss by overshooting their quarry. This results from the fact that deer frequently are closer than archers estimate.

Be sure to pick an imaginary spot on the most vital area and concentrate on it. Aim to hit that spot in the heart area.

Other fatal areas, but areas that ordinarily are not aimed at because of their smaller size, include the spinal column, the throat, and the brain

Fig. 6–9. Virgil Healy, former Indiana State Target Archery Champion, shows Paul Kelly where to aim for a heart shot. "Drive the arrow forward in this spot," he explained.

cavity above and behind the eyes. The large artery lying along the underside of the backbone is particularly fatal when severed.

Rather than risk a shot into the middle of the paunch, one should pass up such shots. Hits in this area result in too extensive a trailing job for a novice, except when a good tracking snow is present. Aim to hit so that your job of retrieving will be less difficult.

An important point in scoring a most effective hit is to pass up your first chance for an oncoming and/or a broadside shot and wait for an opportunity to place your shaft diagonally forward into the chest. Such a strike offers increased opportunity to cut blood vessels, resulting in increased bleeding. The advantage of such a hit was recognized early in bowhunting history. Such a hit is more likely to keep the arrow in the wound where it can continue to cut during the first few jumps of the animal. Another point in favor of refraining from shooting until the animal has passed is that it is far less likely to see you draw your bow for the shot.

IT'S A HIT

When your broadhead is sped on its way to the mark, "follow through" in your shooting form just as you do in good field-shooting form. Good shooting form is just as important in hunting as it is in practice or competitive shooting. After all, isn't this the big moment you have been working up to, to be a successful big-game hunter? Remain absolutely motionless until after the arrow has hit. Concentrate your vision on the animal to see the exact spot where the broadhead hit. Watch the action of the deer carefully. It may provide a clue to the effectiveness of the hit.

If the animal drops in its tracks, that is the signal for shooting it again as *quickly as possible*. This is the *only condition* under which it is proper to get closer in a hurry and to score a second hit—a sort of coup de grâce. The reason for this closing in and rapid delivery of a second arrow is that if an arrow hits any part of the neckbone or backbone, even one of the long dorsal bony processes, the animal is likely to drop in its tracks; however, if the hit is only on one of the dorsal projections of the backbone, the animal will usually regain its feet and be gone within a few fleeting seconds. A hit in such a place that does not keep the deer down from the start may result in endless tracking and searching to recover the animal. A hit above the backbone produces a slow-bleeding wound, resulting in a longer search to find your deer. A direct hit on the solid section of the vertebral column or on the brain case may keep the animal down for good.

If the animal you drop is a bear, do not betray your location but continue to do your additional shooting from concealment if at all possible. It will be safer that way. Since an arrow kills entirely by bleeding and not by shocking power, an arrow-hit bear or cougar has plenty of time to inflict fatal wounds on the archer, even after it has been hit in the heart.

In about ninety-nine cases out of a hundred, a deer will run from the site after it has been hit by an arrow. In each of the six instances when one of the authors bagged whitetailed deer, they dashed away on a "dead" run. Three were hit in the heart, two through both lungs, and one through the liver. In each case, the animal ran as if it had not been injured in any way. The animals, however, seemed to run low to the ground with little or no bound. The gait of some seemed like that of a scared cat that literally skims the ground with a dog snapping at its tail. The general impression created in each case was that the victim ran with its tail down. However, as a result of excitement, or maybe "buck fever," a lot of details went unnoticed.

When a big-game animal is hit and runs from the site, you have to exercise extreme self-control in order to stay put and let the animal go undisturbed for the time being. Letting it go, however, is added insurance for a quicker recovery.

Mark your shooting position by sticking an arrow upright in the ground. Of course, if you shoot from a blind, that extra precaution will be unnecessary. Now take a good look at the landscape, memorizing where the deer stood and exactly where it ran and disappeared from sight. Remember this "picture" well. It may save you much time in retrieving your deer. Now stay put and calm your nerves. This is where your pounding heart and jumpy nerves need a rest anyway.

When you have mastered your excitement, it is time to go to where the deer stood. Mark that spot also by sticking a second arrow upright in the ground. Look for signs of blood. If you do not see any, look for your arrow or broken parts of it. Search the immediate area along which the deer fled, but do not follow the trail more than 25 or 30 yards. By examining the immediate blood trail, you may be able to learn whether or not your hit was a "good" one.

A big-game animal when well hit will usually run but a short distance, seek cover, and lie down. If undisturbed, it will remain there thinking it has eluded its source of disturbance. Loss of blood and/or physiological shock results in rather prompt death, which will get you a trophy. In order to provide the best assurance that a not-so-well-hit deer will go into shock (ordinarily referred to as stiffening up), it is best not to go after your animal for about an hour. This length of waiting is to provide doubly good assurance that the deer can be found at the first spot it lay down. If an animal is rushed too soon, it may still have the ability to move on and hide in thicker cover where tracking and recovery will become doubly difficult. Unless you are exceptionally good at stalking and tracking, it will pay you to wait before going to retrieve your quarry. There are exceptions to this rule. In case of an impending rainstorm or where falling snow is rapidly covering the tracks and blood signs, you may have to pursue your animal sooner. You will have to judge the circumstances under which such action is urgent.

Most circumstances call for a delay before setting out to retrieve your deer. Therefore, when you have waited the suggested hour, you may start looking for your animal. If in the meantime you have "sneaked" out and brought a friend to assist you, it seems most advantageous for you to decide on a course of strategy just in case the animal is not dead. One hunter can best "backtrack" out of the area, circle, and carefully approach the vicinity from beyond where the deer disappeared. The approach should be made carefully by stalking. After a prearranged delay of time, the hunter who stayed at the site of the hit should stalk in the general direction the deer fled. He should check for signs of blood, hair, or broken pieces of the arrow, and for likely places in which the deer may have bedded down. He should remember that the deer may have circled to one side and back slightly before lying down, a trick that such animals commonly use so that they can watch their backtrail for enemies.

A bit of kleenex or toilet tissue stuck onto twigs serves well for marking blood trails. The reason for such trail marking is so that if you lose the trail you can back up, note the general direction of the trail, and start all over again.

Six deer taken by one of the authors never made it to cover to lie down after they were hit with an arrow. They passed out on their feet and slid to the end of their trail—one at 40 yards, one at 70 yards, one at 79 yards, one at 90 yards, and one at 125 yards. The sixth collapsed in the open at 220 yards.

Deer killed by bow and arrow in Allegan County, Michigan, were recovered at an average distance of 206 yards from where hit in 1943, 136 yards in 1944, and 211 yards in 1945. It is natural that deer can and will travel a short distance before bleeding out. The actual distance depends on the location of the hit.

Even bullets with their 3,000 foot-pounds of striking force do not always kill instantly. Only seventeen (37 per cent) of the forty-six deer shot by gun in the Allegan antlerless deer season in 1947 dropped in their tracks. The other twenty-nine deer (63 per cent) traveled an average distance of 550 yards. The average distance traveled by all forty-six deer taken with gun was 349 yards with an extreme distance of 3.5 miles. From all this, it is obvious that what really matters is not whether a hunter uses a gun or bow, but that he uses good judgment and holds his shot until he can place it where it will do the most damage.

Some critics have expressed concern over the possibility of a high crippling loss in bowhunting seasons. Facts do not support this fear. In Michigan where 7,700 archers hunted in 1947, eight Department of Conservation Game Area Managers failed to find even one unclaimed arrow-killed deer during 853 hours of field activity in deer habitat. Two dead deer were seen but, when examined, were found to have died from poachers bullets. Obviously, however, there is bound to be some crippling loss, as such is certain to occur in any type of hunting.

Wisconsin game authorities reported there was very little verified evidence of a considerable number of arrow-wounded or later-found dead deer. In the seasons of 1945–1947 when archers bagged a total of 784 legal deer, evidence of 84 unrecovered deer was reported (11 per cent crippling loss); but only 37 (5 per cent loss) were found at a later date. This crippling loss is in line with usual losses in gun seasons.

KEEP LOOKING

If you are sure of a hit, and that means you have positive evidence of a hit (not just imagination), but cannot find your deer, you have a serious responsibility. It is up to you to keep at it until you have exhausted every possibility of recovering your game. This is an obligation every sportsman must face squarely. Bowhunters in general have a good reputation on this score. Let us help maintain that well-earned reputation.

A few tips may help you find your deer. First, note the general size of the animal's hoof prints. Are they two or three fingers wide; are there any odd marks or special shapes that can be recognized in the prints?

There are many who believe that in flat country, a wounded deer will flee into the wind, depending on its sense of smell to warn it of new danger as it runs from the site. As it grows faint, it may change its direction and travel back downwind a short distance and enter a hidden spot to lie down. In such a spot, it can see a pursuer coming from where it first fled and can smell anyone who tries to trail it into its hiding place.

This information was used to locate a deer for a friend. The animal was trailed with the aid of a flashlight. Although the ground was covered with dry leaves, a drop of blood was found at intervals of about 5 to 10 yards. After going about a quarter of a mile, the deer circled downwind about 40 yards where it was found dead.

In steep country, a vitally wounded deer is reported to be most apt to travel downgrade just before death.

Under no circumstances should a hunter claim a hit unless there is definite evidence of such. If you cannot find your arrow or any sign of blood, hunt for the arrow some more. It may be buried under leaves as far as 10 to 15 yards beyond where the deer stood. Do not guess regarding a hit or a miss; make sure. Hunters who go home and claim to have scored a hit, as a half-hearted excuse for not bringing home a deer, are bringing much unjustified criticism on the "sport of man since time began."

A claim of a hit in the absence of a deer to show for it indicates a crippled animal that was not recovered. So far as antibowhunter critics and the general public are concerned, such claims are a sign of wounding. Many a story has floated from ear to ear because some braggart could not face up to going home empty handed and so he invented a story or wishfully thought he might have hit his deer. Had he taken the time to hunt diligently, he probably would have found his arrow with evidence to indicate a hit or a miss. Since most misses go over the deer, do a thorough job of looking well beyond where the deer stood.

One of the authors once hunted over an hour to find an arrow shot at a deer. No evidence could be found to indicate a hit. Not being able to find the arrow, a search was started for the buck, which was finally found 200 yards distant. Not a drop of blood was found until within about 10 yards of where the deer went down. When dressed, the animal was found to have bled internally. It had been hit in the heart, but the tall grass in which it stood when shot had concealed the fact of the hit. Do not give up the search easily; persistence will often be rewarding.

In waiting before pursuing his deer, the bowhunter, where he is hunting in a special bowhunting season or area, can be reasonably sure that no one else will lay claim to his deer. There may be rare exceptions to this rule in some areas with extreme concentrations of bowhunters. A friend once had a deer literally stolen from under his nose. Such thievery has no place in bowhunting, and it behooves archers to bring pressure on such unprincipled individuals. Report the facts of any such thefts to the state and/or national organizations.

There are rare occasions when two individual bowhunters each have hit the same deer. The second hunter did not even know the animal was previously hit, until he tracked and recovered the animal.

The "law of the chase" so far as the courts are concerned is that the one who first subjects the animal to his control in an open season is deemed to have obtained a property right in the game. Ownership at that point goes directly from the state to the hunter. This principle of first to take control —first to legally possess—although the law, is often abused insofar as sportsmanship is concerned. In gun hunting in many states, it has become a matter of who can run the fastest to be the first to get his seal affixed to the downed deer. Such conduct is unworthy of the sport.

If you down a deer and find part of another hunter's arrow in its body cavity, there is not the slightest doubt as to what you as a true bowhunting sportsman should do. Try to find out whose arrow it is and deliver the carcass to him. Such action will make you a far bigger sportsman in the eyes of the public than if you bagged a dozen deer all by yourself. The Golden Rule certainly applies to the situation. See that the other hunter gets what is logically his. Similarly, if you see a wounded deer, dispatch it at once and then help get it to the rightful owner. That is the only humane and decent thing to do.

If the deer you down has been hit previously, but has only a superficial flesh wound inflicted by another hunter, that poses a somewhat different problem. There are advocates of the "first blood" theory for ownership. It is one way to avoid conflict of interest and ownership and takes real sportsmanship on the part of the hunter who downed the animal. There are circumstances, however, where such a rule is not necessarily the most just. For instance, if a hunter only inflicts a superficial flesh wound high in the neck, on a leg, or on the ham, he has little chance of recovering the animal. Such a wound will heal cleanly and quickly. A second hunter shooting a broadhead and killing such an animal has as good as done it single handedly.

Certainly the man who drew first but superficial blood in such a case would have nothing to be proud of, whereas the second hunter would have good reason for pride. A superficial wound provides poor grounds for priority in ownership. An archer is not showing the highest degree of sportsmanship when he claims ownership on the basis of such a hit. Perhaps the best solution where disputed ownership occurs would be for the two hunters to shake hands across the trophy animal and flip a coin to see who takes the deer and all the honors that go with it. So far as the meat and the hide are concerned, they can split them half and half.

Most hunters occasionally get a deer, but it takes a real sportsman to offer his fellowman the animal when there is some doubt about ownership. A man with sportsmanship enough to give up his claim should receive real consideration for the N.F.A.A. Good Sportsmanship Award.

The fun is in the chase. The minute you lay claim to a deer, your fun is over. Therefore when you offer your fellow hunter the carcass in question, his fun is over. The privilege and pleasure of more hunting remains yours to further enjoy.

7

Tips for More Productive Bowhunting

WHEN TO SHOOT

The deer has exceptional ability to scent a hunter and very keen ears to hear his approach. The hunter frequently does many things wrong or neglects doing things he should do. Any one of these wrong things is enough to prevent his shooting a deer, which always takes advantage of the hunter's mistakes. All of this is true of gun hunters, but it is particularly true of bowhunters since they must get close enough to the deer to make a clean kill. The average distance at which deer are taken with the bow and arrow is approximately 30 yards. If an archer is to hit a deer at any distance, he must do nothing wrong. For many it takes years of trial-and-error experience to learn what these errors are and how to correct or prevent them. In order that the reader may profit by mistakes frequently made, a few bowhunting experiences of archers will be related, each one of which might easily be the cause of failure to come home with a deer.

One archer's first deer hunting experience with the bow, in fact his first deer hunting experience of any kind, was in Westchester County of New York in the fall of 1945. It was a beautiful day and he was thoroughly enjoying still-hunting alone over the lovely rolling country. Suddenly he was alerted by the shrill cry of a bluejay. Then, at least, the archer did the right thing. He stopped, "froze," and stood perfectly still for a while. A bluejay may thus announce the approach of deer, bear, fox, or other game; or he may be startled by you and in this way alert the deer of your presence. After a few very long moments, the archer started a slow careful stalk, moving into the wind as before and gradually climbing up a small rounded and barren hillock. At this point, he did another correct and important thing. He got down on his stomach and slowly crawled up the remaining part of the hill so as to present to possible deer on the other side of the hill the smallest possible object on its horizon over the hill. As the archer slowly and gradually inched his eyes over the edge of the hill to see what was on the other side, he was rewarded by seeing a very large doe reaching her head high to pull down branches of white cedar on which she was munching, unaware of the archer's presence. She was not over 30 to 35 yards away and presented a challenging broadside shot.

While watching the deer, a clump of trees was noted on the right about 15 to 20 yards from the doe. The thought came to the archer that if he could just back down and stalk around to the right and come up behind that clump of trees, he could make his shot from less than 20 yards. With this thought in mind, he slowly inched his head down (and whatever else of him might have been visible to the deer over the rim of the hill) and crawled back around to the right on hands and knees. Then keeping the clump of trees between him and where the deer had last been seen, the archer got to the trees and slowly stood up with bow and arrow at the ready. He looked toward the cedars expecting to see the doe there but was startled by a sharp explosive "HAW!" from the deer, which was now behind him and 40 yards away, waving her flag goodbye as she disappeared into the woods. What actually happened will never be known. Probably the wind changed, or a current of air from the hill with the archer's scent shifted the deer's way. One thing seems sure. The archer should have taken the broadside shot at the deer when first seen feeding on cedar. The archer should have known that the odds would be against his getting closer for a better chance to shoot.

On still another time in New York's Cortland County in 1954 while walking to his stand in the early morning, a cautious peep over the top of a hill revealed a deer grazing 35 or 40 yards away. Again thinking that he might be able to get closer by backing down and circling around more into the wind, the archer slowly eased down to try this. Unfortunately, a deer he had not seen farther to the left took off and spooked the deer first seen and two more. In each of these cases, it would seem that the wrong thing done was failing to take a shot when the deer were first seen at a reasonable shooting distance. Perhaps the lesson taught by these deer was: *One should try a shot if one has an opportunity within 35 yards (or at whatever distance he feels confident in being able to make a killing shot).* The chances for stalking for a closer shot are small.

On another occasion, the day was bitter cold with a steady wind and the rain had changed to sleet. The archer's partner had become chilled and left for the car and its heater. Stubbornly, the archer continued to hunt, starting down over the ridge of the mountain in the general direction of the road with the sleet in his eyes and the noise of it all around. A clump of Staghorn Sumac, mostly dead, reared bonelike skeletons 35 or 45 yards away, adding their chill to the scene. What wonderful camouflage for the rack of a big buck. Then the archer saw a rack of about 6–6 points blending beautifully with the dead sumacs. Thinking about lesson No. 1 and that he ought to shoot since experience had shown the chances were not good for getting a closer shot, the archer aimed for a spot in back of the head and neck directly below the middle of the rack and loosed the arrow. The arrow went a little high, right through the middle of the buck's rack without even hitting a tine. In a flash, the deer and two previously unseen does were out of range down the hill. Possibly the archer was too cold to think straight, or possibly he was experiencing a bit of "buck fever," but he had done at least two things wrong. First, he had forgotten to aim lower than usual since the shot was downhill a little; and second (and this was the exception to lesson No. 1), his situation offered perhaps the best chance he might ever have to stalk closer for a killing shot. The conditions were perfect because the deer were facing the wind and sleet and looking downhill away from the archer. The sleet was making so much noise all the time that the deer could not hear the archer's approach. The archer felt he might have approached the deer as close as 10 yards for the shot that he hurriedly made at 40 yards.

Possibly a second principle is here evolved: *Under favorable conditions of wind, rain, sleet, or snow, and the deer unaware of the hunter, the archer, before taking his shot, may stalk to a position closer than he ordinarily would take.*

DO NOT BE TOO COMFORTABLE

Another time in Michigan's famed Allegan Forest, an archer sat on a tree stump on the side of a hill 20 yards from the top of the ridge with bow and arrow ready. Twenty yards below him, a woods road stretched from side to side; and below that the wooded hill sloped farther and farther downward. The archer could command a view of 270 degrees and was expecting the possibility of deer coming up the hill and crossing the road in front of him. After about 20 minutes of waiting, a stamping noise was heard directly above and behind the archer. There occurred two or three stamps, then perfect quiet. Then the stamping recurred and then as suddenly stopped. The archer had been too comfortable with his weight too far back on the stump. Slowly he leaned forward trying to inch himself toward the front of the stump to bring his weight forward enough to balance it on his feet, his heart pounding as though it would burst. The deer appeared to be headed down the hill to cross the road toward the deeper lowland woods. It could not see the archer but apparently had scented him and was testing him, trying to get him to betray his location by moving. The archer's heart was pounding out the strain of waiting, and he was trying to move slowly enough not to be noticed, but he was "on dead center." He had to rock forward still more to get his weight balanced on his feet, and in doing so revealed his location. The deer's caution had "paid off."

It saw the archer move and wheeled back over the hill before the archer could turn and shoot.

This deer pointed out another lesson: *When on the watch, whether sitting or standing, your weight should be so balanced on both feet that you can pivot evenly and slowly enough to get into position for a shot in any direction of the compass (360 degrees), for deer are where you find them.*

CONSISTENT NOCKING

Archer Jim missed a chance to shoot at either of two deer that jumped from their beds 10 yards from him because as he raised his bow the arrow nock was whisked off the string by a small shrub. Had there been two knots of thread wound around the serving of the string, one immediately above and one just below the nocking point to hold the arrow in place, Jim would at least have had a good shot. Some archers prefer just one knot of string wrapped around the string just above the nocking point. With this system one can place the arrow nock on the string and quickly slide it up against the knot without taking his eyes off the game.

KNOW WHAT YOUR ARROWS WILL DO

Harry had practiced conscientiously with a new set of field arrows that were 28 inches long. He was hitting very well on roving and field targets at distances up to and including 30 yards.

On the first day of the bowhunting season, Harry and Gus stood at their respective stands near deer trails. A doe came along and stopped broadside to Harry 25 yards away. Harry shot his arrow, which was so close it must have parted the deer's hair just under its chest. The doe ran off unscathed. Harry could not understand how he could have missed the deer at such close range until he noted that his hunting arrows were 2 or 3 inches longer and quite a bit heavier than the roving arrows with which he had practiced. This experience drove home the lesson: *One should hunt with arrows as nearly the same length, weight, and spine as those with which he practices.* In fact, one of the hunting arrows from the same set to be used might profitably be shot in practice previous to the hunting trip. Practice with this hunting arrow will dull it and make it unusable for hunting. However, the knowledge gained as to how it shoots and how it may differ in flight from the practice roving arrows (if at all) is well worth the sacrifice of the arrow.

TAKE TIME TO DETERMINE WHERE YOU WILL MAKE YOUR STAND

Archer George had always had so much fun still-hunting for deer that he was generally late getting to his afternoon stand near a likely looking deer trail. On this particular occasion, he and his party had agreed to use the same stands they had used in the morning; and all planned to be back in the neighborhood of these stands by 2:30 in the afternoon.

Having made this decision, they also wisely agreed that their still-hunting and driving would be several miles away from where they would take their afternoon stands so as not to disturb the regular habits of the deer in this area. The driving and still-hunting was carried out as planned, and a few deer were seen but none close enough to tempt a shot.

Promptly at a little before 2:30 P.M., they were back in the vicinity of the stands. For once George felt that he would have enough time to really study the area and determine which spot would be best from which to stand and watch. The area seemed a good one since it was an apple orchard roughly 60 yards in diameter, bordered by the road at the upper end, with pine plantings 20 or more feet high on both sides and at the bottom except where a deer trail funneled down the hill from the middle of the orchard. The trail below the orchard was narrow and bounded by the pine plant-ings. In fact, from the road, three different well-marked deer trails led down through the orchard; and two other trails, one on each side of the orchard and adjacent to the plantings, circled completely around the orchard until all five merged into the one coming from the lower middle part of the orchard to proceed down the hill as one.

George spent nearly a half-hour studying the different trails, the wind direction, and the open spaces, and noting where the droppings were the freshest. He finally chose a stand back to one side where he could command an unobstructed view of all five trails with the wind blowing from the trail toward him; then he waited.

Suddenly without warning and without noise, the head and shoulders of a large doe appeared in front of a blueberry bush on the middle trail headed upwards 25 yards from the archer and on his left. He drew his nocked arrow smoothly back to his anchor and released the shaft. The deer bounded forward, running fast but noisily and in a wide arc to the right. In 3 or 4 seconds, everything was quiet.

George first noted the direction in which the deer was last seen when the noise had stopped. He then left his stand and paced the distance to the spot where the deer had been standing. On the ground just beyond the bush lay the upper or fletched half of the arrow with blood on its broken end.

George then walked back toward his stand and to his surprise found the deer just a few yards from his shooting stand. The arrow had struck just behind the right front leg and had gone through the heart and thorax. It had also cut some of the muscles that pull the right leg back, resulting in shorter strides by that leg, which caused the deer to circle to the right.

The archer cleaned his deer and had it at the edge of the road before five o'clock, when the car with the other men arrived.

BOWSTRING NOISE

An archer who is only average in accuracy, if a fair chance exists, should get within 30 yards of his deer before he shoots. At this close range, there are several factors that can interfere with a successful shot. Some of these have to do with bowstring noise, which warns the deer of impending danger and allows it ample time to jump away before the arrow strikes. In a third of a second, a deer can hear the twang of the string and move away before the arrow can travel 17 yards. This is really lightning-like reaction, but it has happened to many archers including the writers.

The high-pitched twang of a light bowstring is annoying in hunting, and many a deer's "hide" has been saved by the noise of the string. A reasonably heavy string not only reduces string "twang" but adds safety margin in case a briar cuts a strand or two. To dampen or reduce string slap, some hunters wrap strands of soft wool yarn on the outer ends of the string that strikes the recurved bow tips. Others thread rubber gadgets onto the string and place them toward the outer segment of the free part of the string to reduce the vibration causing the high-pitched noise. The round rubber "brush buttons" placed on bowstrings by some archers reduce string slap considerably in addition to keeping twigs and weeds from snagging in the sharp angle between the bow tip and the string (Fig. 5–1). Such snagging is a distinct nuisance to the stalking archer, and the noise produced by such snagging is a warning to deer that an intruder is near.

A properly elevated elbow (rolled outward and upward out of the way) will reduce string slap against the armguard, thereby removing another source of warning to deer.

On a frosty still morning at daylight when not a breath of air is blowing, and not a leaf rustling, a deer can hear the "scraping" of an arrow as it is drawn back on a solid arrow-rest. This "giveaway" has "cheated" many a bowhunter of his deer. For this reason, every hunting bow should have a soft piece of buckskin or fur on the arrow-rest and bow where the arrow makes contact. This will eliminate the rasping friction noise.

If you fail to take precautions against these unnecessary sources of noise, you will probably return a sadder and wiser hunter. To be sure, not all deer will jump at the sudden twang of a string, or the scraping of an arrow, but those that have been alerted to danger in the vicinity will react in a flash. Why not improve your chances for success by eliminating common causes of failure?

CAMOUFLAGING YOUR BOW

Many a bowhunter has returned without a deer because his shiny bow produced reflections that alerted deer far ahead. Bright surfaces are foreign to deer habitat. For successful hunting, they should be eliminated.

If your bow is to be used primarily for hunting, paint it an olive drab color to camouflage it permanently. In any event, the least you should do is to cover it with "camouflage socks," a narrow tube of olive drab knit material that can be stretched over each limb and taped in place. Dark-colored masking tape or green grease paint may be used to cover the shiny varnished surface on a temporary basis. Such paint is now sold by archery dealers under the name of "camouflage stick," with one end consisting of green and the other a tan shade.

CAMOUFLAGE CLOTHING

For success in bowhunting for deer, one must remain hidden from sight as well as from the hearing and the sense of smell of deer. By remaining absolutely motionless, one can usually escape being seen. However, since a hunter frequently wishes to still-hunt or stalk deer, or because he has to move to shoot, it is usually to the hunter's advantage to be well camouflaged (Figs. 7–1 and 7–2).

Fig. 7–1. Comfort as well as concealment is important in deer hunting. On public lands or on private areas where permission may be secured, a blind often can be improved by digging a hole about 2 feet in diameter and a foot deep. With your feet in the hole, you can sit comfortably on the bank and watch for deer on the runway on the upwind side. Such a low position provides additional concealment and easy observation of moving deer in woods.

Fig. 7–2. A well-camouflaged bowhunter points to evidence that he is on a travel lane of a buck. The white newly barked area indicates antler rubbing during the current season. The older brown scars indicate antler rubbing during the previous fall. Archie Bilyeu of Joice, Iowa, decided that this was a good place to start hunting.

Camouflage coveralls and two-piece suits are available, and the use of such clothing is recommended wherever the archery deer season is separate from the gun season. A two-piece suit is preferable because it is less bothersome to remove. Buy a suit considerably larger than you normally use, especially if it is to be used in the colder sections of the country where it will need to fit over heavy clothing.

The use of footgear that blends with the area is essential. White tennis shoes and/or white socks are a giveaway to the still-hunter. As he sneaks along, the part that is most readily seen by the deer as it peers under or through the brushy cover will be the movement of light-colored foot gear as it is flashed with each step. Watch a novice deer hunter sometime, and you will see what is meant.

A camouflage cap or hat, or one adorned with leaves or weeds, will round out the camouflage clothing.

To mask their faces, some hunters streak them with camouflage paint; others smear them with moist earth or a piece of charred wood from an old burned stump or log.

If the hunter is a nervous smoker type who cannot help moving his hand up and down to puff on a cigarette, he should also camouflage his hand.

In approaching an area where deer are expected, or when sitting and waiting for a deer to come to you, you can partly hide your face by holding your bow in such a way that it masks your face so that one eye looks on either side of the bow. In effect, this divides your face in two parts as seen from the deer's position. A weed carried in your hand or teeth so that you look through it also adds camouflage.

When the hunter resorts to all these camouflage tactics, he is equipped to fool most deer that are not in a position to hear or scent him. But such camouflaging is not recommended when one hunts in the regular gun season for deer. To do so is not safe.

A deer, except an occasional "rut-happy" buck, will detour around an area "heavy" with human scent. A wise hunter can use this knowledge to his advantage. If a novice hunter sits in such a position that his scent might turn deer traveling through an area, place yourself in a position to take advantage of any such detouring deer. A tree blind might work well in such a case, as your scent will be up high enough to be dissipated before it gets to any deer.

Special scents to attract deer might be used on a bush or other object to attract a deer's attention away from the bowhunter at a spot where a good shot can be executed.

By adopting these hints for better bowhunting, your chances for success will be improved. You will then be in a position to outsmart and bag even some of the wiser old bucks.

HOW TO SHARPEN YOUR BROADHEADS

Sharp broadheads are a must and can be produced with the use of an ordinary 6-inch metal file, an item that should be included in every bowhunter's paraphernalia. The important technique in the sharpening process is the pattern of stroking the edge of the blade with the file. The direction of each stroke should be parallel to the shaft and from the back toward the tip of the broadhead. Such file strokes are alternated from side to side so as to reduce chances of forming a "feathered" edge, which hinders the creation of a truly sharp edge. Through alternate stroking you can produce an edge that is sharp enough to scrape wetted hair from the back of your hand. When stroking your finger backward along such an edge, you should feel a series of very fine teeth digging into the skin. A finely serrated edge will do an excellent job of cutting tissues and arteries.

A broadhead shot even once should be regarded as dulled and must be resharpened before used to hunt big game (Fig. 7–3).

Fig. 7–3. Sharp broadheads improve chances for retrieving your big-game animal because they increase penetration even when bone is hit. Here O. C. Tisdale, past Alabama Field Archery Champion, is putting a keen edge on his broadheads for the coming day's hunt.

The advantage of a sharp-edged broadhead for big-game hunting is recognized by experienced hunters. They know that such an arrow, if it does not pass completely through the animal on the initial strike, will continue its mission of cutting vital arteries during the short flight of the animal. In case of a non-vital flesh wound, such an arrow will soon work its way on through, leaving a clean cut to heal.

STALK FOR PRACTICE

Success in stalking is important not only in bagging big game, but also in the enjoyment that such activity can produce. The biggest barrier to successful still-hunting and stalking comes from the "buck fever" that interferes with good reasoning performance at the crucial moment for shooting. The best way to overcome such handicaps is to practice stalking game for the mere fun and experience of it and without a weapon. This can lengthen the season of fun in hunting to a 12-month basis. You will be amazed at what you can learn about animals through still-hunting and stalking without a weapon with only a camera in your hands. The proof of your success will be your closeup photograph of the animal. Your photo will be comparable to a "coup feather" in the Indian brave's coup stick, a symbol of success in the face of great odds against success. One way the Indian could earn such a feather of distinction was to be able to approach and touch his enemy and escape without killing him. Such a feat warranted great recognition for the brave. Your closeup photo of a wild deer may become your "coup feather."

Once you have successfully stalked game and/or purposely have passed up shots at game at close quarters, you will be much more adept at planning your shots so as to do your shooting when you are least apt to get caught at it, and when you have the deer in the best possible position for a well-placed hit. To be able to do so will reduce crippling losses and will cut down on the effort needed to retrieve your deer. A bowhunter owes it to his sport to be able to withhold his shot until he can place his arrow where it will be most lethal. This can be done only through know-how and experience. A successful bowhunter has taken the time to gain both.

8

Safety in Bowhunting

If a person is to get lasting pleasures and recreation out of bowhunting, it must be done safely. Nothing can wreck the success and pleasures of a hunting trip more than getting one's self lost, getting injured, or causing injury to someone else. Such misfortunes involve not only the hunter but also his hunting companions, and friends, and family back home. It behooves each bowhunter to learn good safety habits and to familiarize himself with proper procedures to follow in case of emergencies. This chapter is written with these points in mind.

Daniel Boone is reported to have said that he was never lost, but that one time he was turned around for 2 or 3 days. Bowhunters also occasionally get turned around, especially when hunting in strange areas. The suggestions that follow should help keep hunters from becoming lost; but for those that still blunder and lose their way, the suggestions may help keep them safe and reasonably comfortable until a searching party can come to their rescue.

ITEMS FOR YOUR SAFETY

Maps, though not necessary where one hunts on farmland or in woodlots, are particularly useful for hunting in wildland areas. The safest practice when hunting on wildland is to know the lay of the land of the area you intend to hunt, or to hunt with someone who does. When you have decided on the area, unless you are quite familiar with it, get topographical maps of the vicinity. Get them from whatever local vendor supplies them, or order them direct from the U. S. Geological Survey, Washington, D.C. Cloth can be glued to the back of your map to make it more durable. Fold your map in such a way that the area you intend to hunt is on the outside and insert it in a transparent plastic envelope to keep it clean and in good condition. Carry it in your hunting coat for quick reference in the field.

If your hunting site is in a National Forest, you will find it to your advantage to stop at the forest headquarters and ask to see their aerial photograph of the area. Most forest headquarters have such photos. Your time spent examining such photos will be well repaid because it will give you ideas about areas with cover conditions worth hunting.

94

Survival and/or comfort may depend on such important items as matches in a waterproof container, a dependable compass, a sharp pocket knife (or a 6-inch blade sheath knife), a police whistle (or shotgun shell) for producing whistle signals, a first aid kit, a thin plastic raincoat, a lunch, and emergency rations. The bowhunter will also be wise to carry a few halazone tablets for sterilizing drinking water and some aluminum foil for making a drinking cup.

THINGS TO DO FOR YOUR SAFETY

Maps to be most useful to the hunter must be related to the land features in your hunting area. When you have selected your campsite or headquarters from which to hunt, lay your map on the ground and orient it with regard to true directions and local land features. This is done by placing your compass on the map and then rotating the map until its vertical edge is in line with the compass needle and the top of the map is pointing the same direction as the north end of the compass needle.

Maps normally are printed with north at the top unless otherwise indicated. Note the number of degrees of angle declination generally printed at the bottom of the map, then shift the edge of the map that same number of degrees until it is properly aligned for true north. The map is now oriented for use. Its direction of features now correspond with the lay of the land.

Study the lay of the land in relation to the map. Note well and memorize unusual or outstanding land features. Mark them on your map if you can. Now mark the spot corresponding to the location of your camp or base of operations. Knowing the relation of one's campsite to landmarks may not keep everyone from getting lost, but it will certainly help get the wandering individual back to camp if his wandering brings him back within sight of one of the landmarks.

If the area is strange to you, ask questions of the persons most familiar with the lay of the territory. If you know most about it, brief the others. Discuss the locations of roads, fire lanes, and their direction and distance away; locations of swamps and streams, if present; and direction of stream flow. Prevailing directions of ridges and the wind are also useful bits of information.

These items may seem petty and unnecessary to some members in the party; but to one who is in new country, they will be most welcome information. Perhaps the person who needs the information most is too timid to ask. Sharing such information with such an individual may save you hours of effort and anxiety trying to find him if he should get lost. To be forewarned is to be forearmed.

Establish a base line of operations in relation to your camp. This is especially desirable when hunting for the first time in extensive wildland territory. Such a base line is much easier to establish if you take the pains to locate your camp where it can be seen from a road, a river, a fire lane, or some similarly prominent landmark. Before the archers new to an area do any extensive hunting, they should explore and become familiar with the area along this line for a few miles in each direction from the camp. They can do so by still-hunting in the habitat along the base line (creek, road, etc.). Firsthand knowledge of the features along this line will make it possible for one to quickly recognize his whereabouts whenever he crosses the line in more serious hunting activity in days to come. Such knowledge of the territory not only is comforting, but makes it possible to devote greater attention to the job of stalking game.

Blazing a trail from a remote hidden camp to a well-recognized base line or trail can be useful in wildland areas. In making such blazes, it may be well to make the marks higher up on the side of the tree toward camp and lower down on the side away from camp.

Check your compass at regular intervals while hunting so as to keep properly oriented. Notice landmarks, direction and/or changes in wind or air currents, direction of flow of streams, time of day and the remaining hours of daylight. You will want to be back in camp by dark.

If without a compass (you should not be unless you lost it), you should know how to determine directions by means of common sense. It is helpful to know that in the northern half of the United States and Canada, the sun is in the south from about 10:30 A.M. through 2:30 P.M. If the sun is out enough to cast a shadow during this period of the day, an east-west direction line can be determined from watching the line of travel of the tip of the shadow from a 5- or 6-foot stick set upright or from a tree snag on level ground. Merely mark the position of the exact tip of the shadow by placing a twig at that point. Wait 10 or 15 minutes and then mark the new position of the tip of the shadow. A line between the two points where the shadow tips were marked is the east-west line.

Tell the other hunters or leave a written note indicating where you expect to hunt before returning. Each evening, archers may find it advantageous to plan how and where they expect to hunt the following day. Such planning will contribute to a most enjoyable hunt.

IF LOST, WHAT THEN?

In spite of the best laid plans, there may come a time when a bowhunter becomes "confused" and not know in which direction camp lies. He is lost and feeling very lonely. A friend of the authors got lost at dusk one rainy evening in Kentucky. When his flashlight failed, he took out his hunting knife and made shavings for kindling from one of his cedar arrows. But alas, all his matches had become soaked by the rain. He spent a miserable night with freezing temperatures doing pushups to keep warm in his wet clothes. He had the good sense to keep from panic and stayed in one place throughout the hours of darkness. If he had carried his matches in a waterproof container, he could have been comfortable all night, even though lost.

One of the most important things for a lost hunter to remember is to remain calm. He must guard against panic, which might cause him to dash blindly off in any direction. He probably should sit down for 10 or more minutes and take stock of his situation. He should blow three long blasts on the whistle he brought for such an emergency and repeat the whistling at about 5- to 10-minute intervals. Someone may hear him and answer. The type of signaling should have been agreed upon ahead of time by the party of hunters. If no one answers and the sun is getting low with only about an hour of daylight remaining, then the lost hunter better prepare to spend the night where he is and to make preparations so as to make it as comfortable for himself as possible. It certainly is not good sense to stumble around in the woods after dark. To do so may result in a broken leg.

The lost hunter should look for a safe spot to build a fire. This might be on a broad flat rock or on the edge or in the bed of a dry stream. The humus and duff on a suitable area may be removed from an 8- to 10-foot diameter area for a safe campfire site. While there is still daylight, he should gather plenty of firewood (avoid wood with poison ivy on it) for the night and then build a windbreak of logs and boughs of shrubs or trees. Such a windbreak will also serve to reflect some heat, which may be particularly useful in the northern climates. A pile of 6- to 8-inch tips of branches broken from the boughs of balsam fir and/or hemlock, where available, will make a reasonably comfortable bed for the night. The plastic raincoat carried will come in handy to serve as a windbreaker and to keep him dry if it should rain.

After dark the hunter should use dry wood on the fire to produce bright flames that may be seen farther at night. He should get what sleep he can and put more wood on the fire each time he awakens or finds the fire in need of additional fuel. At daylight, ferns, grass, or damp weeds should be added to the fire so as to produce a thick smoke that can be seen a long ways. Three blasts on the whistle at regular intervals should be followed by intent listening for a possible reply from a hunting buddy or searching party.

If his friends have not found him by about eight o'clock the next morning, he may now start out in whatever direction he thinks is most likely to lead back to camp, going slowly and blazing his trail as he goes so as to make it possible to find his way back to the camp where he spent the night, if he needs to return there to rebuild his signal fire. Marking the trail can be done in several ways: by bending branches of shrubs and trees down every few steps, dropping branches in his trail with butt ends pointing the way he is going, or overturning moss to expose black earth at 8- to 10-pace intervals.

After blazing or marking a trail in one direction for a mile or so, he should backtrail to his overnight camp and again build up the fire to make more smoke. After resting a while, he should start out in the next most logical direction, again marking his trail. There is no need for hurry. Saving energy and not going too far from the smoke-producing fire is most important. Keep in mind that it is important to make it easy for friends to spot the smoke and thereby find the lost hunter. Smoke from the campfire and regular series of whistle signaling will help a great deal.

The earlier suggestion of keeping from getting lost in the first place is most imortant. If you fail to keep that advice, then let us hope you memorize what to do if and when the panicky feeling of getting lost hits you. You will feel like starting to run in almost any direction and your tongue will feel as if you had not had a drink for a long, long time. If this situation hits you, it is time to use your head, even if you did not do so up to that moment.

FIRST AID SUPPLIES

First aid supplies are needed by hunters who remain in the woods for more than 1 day at a time. No matter how well you feel when you leave home, there is a possibility that someone in your camp may become ill or suffer accidental injury. It is far better to be prepared than to be sorry. Items that should be included in your kit are laxative pills, unguentine ointment, rubbing alcohol, aromatic spirits of ammonia (one teaspooonful to one-half glass of water for a stimulant), aspirin, iodine, adhesive tape, bandaids, a roll of gauze bandages, three triangular bandages, talcum powder (corn starch may be substituted, for skin rash), and a first aid booklet. A bar of yellow old-fashioned strong laundry soap (if you can find one) may be useful if anyone in the party is sensitive to poison ivy.

Do not forget to double check on the locations where pressure on an artery will control bleeding in extremities. A pocket hand-warmer may double for use to help keep you comfortable on the deer stand and for applying heat to aching muscles that may have become accidentally overtaxed. Do not forget to take along a supply of cough drops. They may be useful for relief from cough both in camp and on the deer stand. Coughing while hunting is certain to warn deer within hearing that an intruder is present and that it is time to sneak away.

For safety, inform your companions where you expect to hunt each day so that in case of accidental injury, they may know where to look for you if you fail to return.

ACCIDENTAL INJURIES AND DEATH ARE AVOIDABLE

"I could hear the doctor tell the nurses I didn't have a chance to live. I had sunk so low I couldn't give a sign of life and I didn't care what they said." So spoke a luckless bowhunter interviewed in a hospital in Michigan in 1946. One of his own hunting companions had shot him for a deer one dusky evening. His partner had heard rustling of leaves behind a distant bush, had drawn his bow, and waited until he caught a glimpse of movement emerging from behind a bush. As soon as the arrow was on its way, and too late to do anything further, it was realized the intended victim was a man and not a deer. The arrow struck just below the ribs, creased the stomach, and lodged against the backbone. Luckily, the victim survived, thanks to plasma, blood transfusions, penicillin, and the fact that the arrow missed the major arteries and veins.

This is an example of needless injury. It was really not an accident; it was willful negligence. A year or two later, a similar injury occurred at another area. One case of death from an arrow occurred a few years later when a broadhead shot at a deer on a ridge missed its intended mark, sailed over the hill, and killed a hunter completely hidden from view of the bowhunter who did the shooting. To the authors' knowledge, there have been only two deaths due to bowhunting in modern times. Lesser and self-inflicted injuries, however, are more numerous than necessary.

Accident prevention in the sport of bowhunting is little different from accident prevention in any type of activity; it requires forethought and planning. Although the sport of bowhunting is generally regarded as one of the safest, unnecessary injuries do occur. Accidents associated with the sport may be grouped into four main categories: (1) accidents that are peculiar to the sport of bowhunting, (2) accidents related to hunting or outdoor recreation in general, (3) death from overexertion, and (4) death and injuries from indiscretion on the highways in traveling to and from hunting areas. Now let us examine more closely some of the causes of accidents.

ACCIDENTS PECULIAR TO BOWHUNTING

The possibility of shooting one's self is one hazard that is practically non-existent in bowhunting. However, the bow and the broadheads provide new and novel ways for inflicting injury. The greatest source of injury is in careless handling of arrows and thereby cutting one's self with the broadhead. Some precautions to observe include:

1. Do not jump a ditch or step on a brush pile with an arrow on the string or in the hand.
2. Do not walk with an arrow on the string with a hunting companion walking on the same side on which you are carrying the bow. Your arrow may stick him in the leg.
3. Do not leave broadheads where children can get at them.
4. Do not throw broadheads loose on the seat of a car; keep them in a quiver. If they are kept in a bow quiver, keep a cloth wrapped around the head end when not in use.

5. Do not draw your hunting shaft on the bow unless you intend to shoot.
6. Do not shoot broadheads at squirrels or game birds directly overhead. The victim may be yourself. Flu flus should be used for such hunting.
7. Do know exactly what you are shooting at and that the arrow will not cause injury to someone in case you miss.
8. Do file broadheads sharp by stroking from the base of the head toward the tip. It prevents sticking your hand while filing.
9. Do keep companions away from the proximity of the upper limb of the bow while stringing the weapon. A bow limb that slips from your hand or as the string slips from the nock may punch out an eye or crack a skull.
10. Do discard any arrow showing a cracked shaft, and do so by breaking it on purpose. If shot, such an arrow may break in the process of shooting and pierce the shooter's hand.

ACCIDENTS RELATED TO HUNTING OR RECREATION IN GENERAL

A well-informed and properly equipped sportsman can prevent most accidents that are common to all kinds of hunting.

Bowfishing, which is done either while wading or from boats, if it is to be done safely, must be accompanied by good boating manners. Safety precautions normally recommended for fishermen should be observed in order to prevent unnecessary drownings.

Ice on creeks and rivers, although not always the safest means, often provides an avenue for easier stalking or travel to and from hunting spots. Before a hunter uses such avenues for travel, however, he must make certain the ice is thick enough to be safe. The carrying of a long light pole will add safety by providing a means for getting back onto the surface of the ice in case of a breakthrough. Once on top of the ice again, a person can roll away from the hole to reach safety.

Falling branches or trees can be a source of danger, especially at times of high winds. Under such conditions, it is well to avoid areas with dead or decaying timber.

OVEREXERTION IS A KILLER

In bowhunting there is little excuse for racing over hill and dale inviting overexertion. Take it easy! It is more fun and the most productive way to hunt anyway. Since success in bowhunting requires that the hunter must see the deer before it sees him, he should devote his efforts toward stealthy stalking or silent watching along a runway. If a deer is bagged, use discretion in dragging it out. After dragging a 125-lb. deer for a couple of hundred yards, the hunter may feel as if he has been dragging a 250-lb. animal. Take it easy; call for help; someone will be glad to help drag your deer out to the road. There is no need to invite a heart attack.

SAFETY ON THE HIGHWAY

Without doubt, the greatest hazard to the bowhunter is his driving to and from his hunting area. Courtesy and defensive driving and the allowing of ample time for travel at moderate speeds will do much to reduce this hazard. Take your time; do not take unnecessary chances.

The whole program of safety may be summed up in the word itself!

    S   *Sportsmanship*

       A   *Alertness*

          F   *Forethought*

             E   *Easy does it*

                T   *Teach others*

                   Y   *Your life may be at stake*

9

Your Big-Game Animal in Hand

CLEANING FOR BETTER VENISON

An important part of the adventure in bowhunting can be in eating. This, however, depends on how good a job you do in taking care of your game animal once it has been downed. With proper "know-how," cleaning a deer is simple; and venison roasts and steaks can be most appetizing.

The purpose of this section is to pass on information on proper handling of the carcass so you, too, can get the most out of your hunt.

In bowhunting there is no need to be concerned with bleeding the animal when it is found. Actually you did the sticking when your arrow first hit the animal. If the animal drops in its tracks as a result of a hit in the vertebral column or the head, however, sticking is in order. It is safer to do the additional bleeding operation by shooting a second arrow into the heart. If you elect to do the sticking with a knife, approach the downed critter from the back, set one foot firmly on the antler on the ground, or on the head if it is a doe, and reach over the animal's shoulder to do the sticking. Downed deer have been known to kick and break a hunter's leg or to cause other injury by a last desperate swing of the antlers.

Sticking, if done, should be done low in the throat, where it joins the brisket. Slitting the neck from ear to ear or making a jagged cut across the middle of the throat will disfigure the skin and make it difficult for your taxidermist to prepare an attractive trophy mount. Old-time hunters insist on cutting off the buck's reproductive organs at once, insisting that these organs "taint" the meat if left on. Apparently this claim has more basis in superstition than in fact.

There are two sets of glands on the hind legs of deer that may impart an undesirable taste to the meat. The matatarsal gland is on the outside of the shank of the hind leg and is marked by an elongated patch of hair with a white central area (Fig. 9–1). Its secretion has a musky odor. The tarsal gland is marked by a tuft of coarse and longer hairs on the inside of the hock joint. It secretes an oily substance with a strong smell of ammonia. The handling of meat after soiling one's hands with the musky or oily secretions on the hair of these glands may taint the meat. Hunters, there-

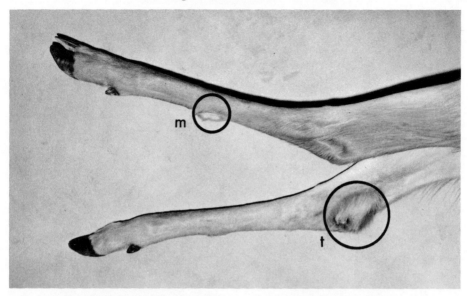

Fig. 9–1. The tuft of longer and dark brown hair on the inside of the hock marks the site of the tarsal (*t*) gland. The secretion from this gland along with the urine that the deer purposely deposits on the hind legs may taint the meat if the hunter is careless enough to contaminate his hands and knife and then spreads it to edible parts while cleaning the animal. The small patch of white hairs on the outside of the hind legs between the hoof and the hock marks the site of the metatarsal (*m*) gland.

fore, commonly cut these glands off. If the glands are removed, it seems most advisable to do so after the deer has been gutted. This procedure will reduce chances of transferring glandular secretions to the meat by way of soiled hands and knife.

Quick cooling of the carcass is desirable. The entrails should be removed as soon as practicable. This job is easily done by the lone hunter armed with no more than a sharp man's-sized pocketknife.

A workable procedure for cleaning a deer is as follows:

1. Make a circular cut around the rectum (Fig. 9–2a).
2. Start at the tip of the breast bone and slit the skin and body wall all the way to the crotch. If the slit is made while the knife is held between two fingers, as illustrated, there will be no chance of cutting the paunch or entrails (Fig. 9–2b).
3. With the deer on its side, pull the entrails from the body cavity, cut around the diaphragm along the ribs, and cut off the gullet and windpipe in the chest cavity (Fig. 9–2c). The rectum can be pulled forward from the circular cut and removed intact with the intestines without further cutting. The lungs should be removed, but the heart may be left in. Save the liver if it looks normal. (There is no need to worry about cutting the gall

bladder as a deer does not have one.) You may want to save the kidneys as many people eat them.

4. Do not throw away meat that is bloodshot. It can be trimmed off and soaked in cold salted water for use in stews.

Fig. 9–2a. To clean a deer: first, make a circular cut around the anus so that the rectal tract can be removed intact with the rest of the entrails.

Fig. 9–2b. Second, make a cut through the skin and abdominal wall from the chest to the crotch.

Fig. 9–2c. Third, with the deer on its side, the entrails are now easily worked out of the stomach cavity. The rectum, which was first cut around, should come out with the large intestines and stomach.

If your deer was shot away from a road, you are now ready to bring it out. If your age is such that you have cause to be concerned about over-exertion, go for help. First, however, take a good look at local landmarks of the area so that you can find it again. If, however, you are young, healthy, and willing, you should now tie to the antlers or head that piece of nylon or sash cord you brought along for this very purpose (or use your bow-string), prop the animal's front feet behind its antlers or head (so they will not catch in the brush), and start dragging your animal out (Fig. 9–3). A friend is really handy at about this point! Do not invite disaster by trying to carry your deer out or you may be mistaken for a deer and shot by another hunter.

When you get the carcass to your car, prop the stomach slit open to allow quicker cooling and put it on a top carrier; in the trunk; or the box, if you drive a truck. Never put your deer on the hood of your car, since heat from the car's engine may cause spoilage.

If your state is one in which conservation authorities operate official deer checking stations, take the carcass to the nearest station where a game biologist or conservation officer will determine age, weight, and other bio-logical data. Such data and materials are being collected to provide a sound basis for deer management. Weight of the deer may reflect food conditions in the area.

If you have a cold storage locker, you are now ready to head for your butcher and let him worry about caring for your animal. The carcass

Fig. 9–3. A nylon cord is excellent for dragging your deer from the field. Cross the animal's front legs behind its neck before attaching the cord so as to prevent their catching on brush and thereby making the dragging more difficult. In the absence of a nylon cord, a bowstring may serve well for dragging out your deer.

should be hung with the hide on in cold storage (at 38° F.) for 2 weeks to properly age the meat. Venison is dry meat and that is the reason for leaving the hide on so as to conserve moisture. Such aging will assure better quality meat. Afterward, skin the animal; and cut, package, and freeze the meat for transfer to your own freezer.

The weight of a deer carcass is reduced by about 20 per cent in removing the paunch (hog dressed). A study in Michigan showed that the fully dressed weight is about 54 per cent of the live weight.

For those who prefer to process their own deer, hang the animal by the hind legs for skinning—like beef. Some sportsmen, however, prefer to hang the animal by its head. Using your knife sparingly and carefully while skinning will help to assure you a good buckskin for tanning.

The usual cuts of meat on a deer carcass are illustrated in Fig. 9–4.

TROPHY ANTLERS AND PRIDE

Trophy heads of game species can be a source of real pride, especially if they are outstanding specimens and are well mounted. Regardless of the outstanding quality of the original specimen, however, mishandling of the trophy head in the field or at any time before getting it to the taxidermist can result in a miserable looking mount. Your taxidermist may be a "whizz" at his profession, but he finds it mighty difficult to cover a jagged cut across the middle of the throat where you may have cut in vain trying

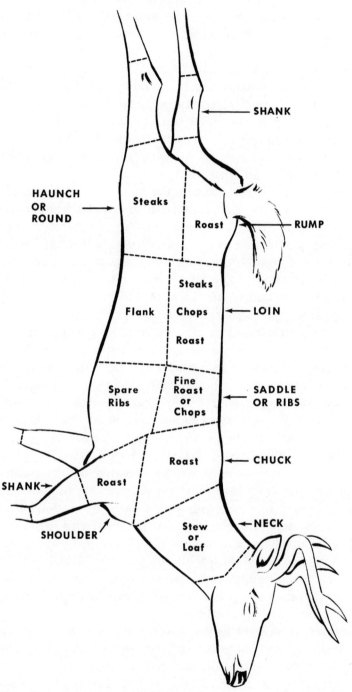

Fig. 9–4. Proper cutting and labeling of the various cuts of meat from your deer will make it possible to select a piece of meat to suit your fancy for various festive occasions.

to get blood out of a dead specimen. He also finds it next to impossible to replace hair you rubbed off the head while dragging the animal a mile or more through brush and over sharp rocks. Similarly, if in the process of skinning you made unnecessary cuts through the skin on the ears and eyelids, or lips, you have compounded his troubles. If you also allowed the skin to lie around in warm temperatures without taking proper care of it so that the hair started to slip, then you have really made a mess of your specimen. Give your taxidermist a chance to do the very best job of preserving trophies. You can help by bringing him quality specimens. Even a taxidermist is proud of an outstanding mount.

If you live near or kill your deer in the vicinity of a taxidermist's shop, take it there without delay. A really fresh unskinned head will give him the best to work with. If the head must be shipped, it can still be sent as an unskinned specimen except in areas where daily temperatures climb above 40° F., such as occurs in the southern states and in areas where hunting seasons are very early in the fall. In the northern states and Canada, hunting season temperatures are such that an unskinned head can be shipped safely, if shipped within 2 or 3 days.

To ship a fresh unskinned head, remove it by cutting the skin at the shoulder, never farther up on the neck. After rinsing off any blood on the hair, it may then be wrapped in burlap and placed in a plastic bag. Now put the wrapped specimen in a burlap bag and place the bundle in a shipping crate. A little excelsior will help pad the antlers and protect the points. By keeping the antlers topmost, there is the least chance that the points will make a hole in the plastic. Be sure to mark the topside of the crate as follows: PERISHABLE—RUSH, THIS SIDE UP. Now ship it express prepaid. Be sure to indicate the contents on the outside of the crate. Since various states have local regulations affecting the transportation of game, be sure to check with your local conservation officer before you ship the specimen. Chances are that the least that will be required of you will be for you to indicate contents, and to record your name, address, and license number on the outside of the package. DO NOT USE PEN AND INK for addressing the crate unless you know definitely that the ink is of permanent type. Use a pencil for addressing the crate, and the writing will still be legible even if the label gets wet.

If the weather in the area in which you hunt or live is warm, or if you desire for other reasons to skin the specimen before shipping, take care to do a good job. Assuming that the skin has been cut at the shoulders, you should next split it up the middle of the back of the neck from the shoulder blades to the antlers as shown in Fig. 9–5. Peel the skin loose from the neck and then sever the ear cartilage as close to the skull as possible. Work the skin loose from around the antlers and down to the eyes. Here you will have to take extra care or you will cut and damage the eyelids. At this

Fig. 9–5. The dotted line indicates the line along which the skin should be cut if the head is to be mounted.

point, keep the cutting edge of the knife working against the bony orbit around the eyesockets. This should get you safely by the eyes. When you get to the lips, again do all the cutting with the knife constantly edging against the jawbones and nose. When skinning around the ears, eyes, and lips, haste definitely makes waste.

When the cape is off the head, you can go back and loosen the cartilage part way up into the ears and remove any loose flesh; but leave the entire ear cartilage attached. The reason for loosening the ear cartilage part way is to permit applying salt to the ear skin to prevent unnecessary slipping of the hair. Now is the time to use a dull knife or scraper to remove any adhering flesh to the inside of the skin.

In order to prevent blood stains on the hair, wash the scalp in cold water. Squeeze out excess water but do not wring the scalp, and hang it over a board or wire to let the excess water drip off. Now thoroughly salt the entire flesh side, making sure that salt gets into every fold. Roll it up, flesh side in, and store in a cool place until the next day when you should work another coating of salt into the flesh by rubbing it in. You can now hang it flesh side out and let it dry in a cool shady place until it is dry enough to be barely pliable enough to permit rolling for shipping.

The skull should also be prepared for shipment, as some taxidermists still use the original skull for mounting. Others may use a papier-mâché skull form to which to attach the skull cap for the mount. Where the skull is to be used, clean off all loose flesh from its outside. The brains can then be flushed out by directing a stream of water from the end of a garden hose nozzle into the vertebral opening at the base of the skull. When all excess tissues have been carved off, hang it up and let it dry for a day. Give it a spraying of insecticide and the pesky flies will be discouraged if there are still any around in your section of the country at this season. Shipping the dried cape and skull with rack will not necessitate the use of a plastic sack in the packing process; otherwise the process is the same as for the fresh specimen. Be sure to attach a letter of instruction. Type it or write it with pencil. Give information on size of the animal, where killed, species, and any special instructions for mounting and shipping the finished specimen.

It goes without saying that if you bag a specimen you believe outstanding and that may qualify for Boone and Crockett Club competition, in the Pope and Young North American Big Game Trophy Competition, or for the N.F.A.A. Prize Buck awards, be sure to contact a qualified representative of one of these organizations in your state. Your State Conservation Office and/or officers of your local archery club or State Association should be able to assist you in this matter.

Measurements for trophy competition must be taken at least 60 days after the animal was killed. This is to permit specimens to completely dry out and to have undergone all possible shrinkage before measurements are recorded.

There is a difference in minimum requirements to qualify for competition in the various big-game records competitions. In general, requirements are highest in the Boone and Crockett Competition. The reason for this is obvious. It has been the gun hunters' trophy club for years, with a selection of the best trophies from hundreds of thousands of big-game animals taken over the decades.

Pope and Young North American Big Game Competition is of recent origin (1957). It is designed to preserve records and to give recognition for outstanding trophies taken by bow and arrow only. Ranking is based on skulls, tusks, horns, and/or antlers of various big-game animals. Principal objectives for Pope and Young Awards are to promote qualitative hunting, to preserve data for record trophies, and to give recognition to hunters bagging outstanding animals.

Qualifying scores for entry in the Pope and Young Competition were set at a realistic level. It was assumed that the minimum scores would have to be low enough so as to provide reasonable chance that a number of bowhunters' trophies could qualify for the competition each year. After all, without reasonable numbers of entries each year, there could be no spirit of competition. Minimum scores for typical racks are as follows:

White-tailed deer	115
Mule deer	135
Columbian black-tailed deer	75
Coues deer	68

Information on other species of big game provided for in the competition may be checked in your N.F.A.A. handbook. For detailed information, write to Glenn St. Charles, Pope and Young Records Committee Chairman, Des Moines, Washington.

If it is a buck deer trophy you have and you do not regard it as quite outstanding enough to qualify for Boone and Crockett or Pope and Young Competition, it may still be a winner in the annual N.F.A.A. Prize Buck Contest. This competition is limited to three species; namely, mule deer, black-tailed and white-tailed deer. To qualify for the contest, you must be a member of the N.F.A.A., so make sure your dues are paid before you go hunting. Winners receive the usual Art Young Big Game Award pin, but with a special diamond mounted therein. Check your N.F.A.A. official handbook or write to the secretary of that organization at Redlands, California, for details.

SAVE-A-BUCK-MOUNT

There are times when a hunter has neither the time, money, nor inclination to have a trophy head made into a conventional mount. Perhaps there are too many "dust catchers" in the house now. Then too, the amount of room required for a Save-A-Buck-Mount is so much smaller that it will fit much better into the small modern-home den.

The specimen is prepared by sawing off the front of the skull along a line from the back of the head to the nose-tip. Do the sawing as shown in Fig. 9–6, removing the antlers, skull cap, and nasal bones intact. The skin, flesh, and other gristle is then removed and discarded. The bony parts of

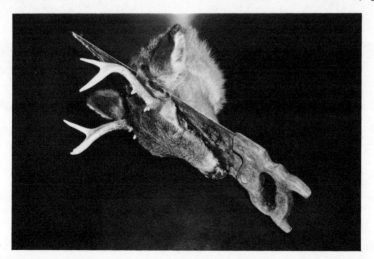

Fig. 9–6. To salvage the skull cap and antlers for a Save-A-Buck-Mount, remove the front part of the skull by sawing along a line extending through the nostrils, through the middle of the eye, and the front edge of the ear.

the skull are then washed clean and soaked in cold water to remove traces of blood. A toothbrush can then be used to apply a solution of chlorox to the bones to bleach them. Do not let the solution get onto the antlers unless you intend to bleach them also, or it will leave spots of whiter antler bone showing. As soon as properly bleached, rinse the skull thoroughly to remove traces of chlorox and let the trophy dry.

Prepare a keystone-shaped mounting board out of ¼-inch plywood, sand it, and apply a coat of flat black enamel. When both the board and the specimen are dry, attach the skullcap with its attached antlers to the mounting board by means of two screws. One screw may be set through each of the naturally occurring holes in the forehead (Fig. 9–7).

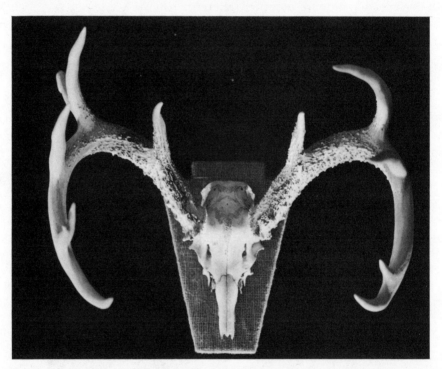

Fig. 9–7. A Save-A-Buck-Mount. The mount is easily made by any do-it-yourself-type individual. Advantages are that it is attractive, low in cost, requires a minimum of room, and leaves little area for dust to collect.

You now have a do-it-yourself-type Save-A-Buck-Mount. This will add another handicraft activity to your bag of archery tricks. It will be fun, just like making a string for your bow, or fletching and painting your own arrows. Such activity is part of the enjoyment of the sport of archery.

10

Hunting Wild Boar, Javelina, and Feral Hogs

Hunting wild European boar with bow and arrow offers top priority in thrilling sport. Any of the wild species of pigs, however, can be dangerous and offer the bowhunter plenty of challenging and exciting sport.

The European wild boar, *Sus scrofa,* was first introduced into the United States in the spring of 1912 when thirteen animals were released on Hooper's Bald in western North Carolina. From here they eventually spread into the adjoining mountains in eastern Tennessee.

The average size of mature wild boars is about 225 lbs. They are armed with formidable tusks (Figs. 10–1 and 10–2) and a thick protective shield of gristle along the side of the neck and chest.

HUNTING THE EUROPEAN WILD BOAR

The first open hunting seasons on wild boar in the United States were in 1936 for Tennessee, and 1937 for North Carolina.

Three different hunting systems are used on wild boar: the "stand," the "still-hunt," and the "chase."

The first archers to hunt European wild boar in the United States used the "chase" method. Since one of the authors, Metcalf, was in this group, he will briefly describe in the first person experiences of hunting wild boar with bow and arrow.

THE FIRST HUNT. We Metcalfs moved to Nashville, Tennessee, in the early summer of 1936, the very year in which the first gun hunting season for wild boar was held in the Cherokee National Forest of Tennessee.

I soon became acquainted with members of the staff of the Tennessee State Department of Conservation and asked permission to hunt wild boar with the bow and arrow. This request was flatly refused with the explanation that it was not possible to kill wild boar except with high-powered rifles. I had different ideas about this but did not press the issue.

In the summer of 1938, I was approached by a representative of the Tennessee Wild Life Association who had heard of my interest in hunting

113

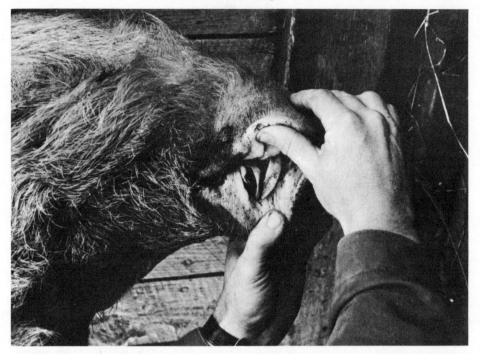

Fig. 10–1. Dr. D. A. Hindman unsheathes the tusks of the 400-lb. wild boar he shot with bow and arrow in Tennessee's Cherokee National Forest. (Tenn. Conservation Dept. photo.)

wild boar with bow and arrow. He told me that if I could locate two other archers with this same interest, he would see to it that the three of us had our chance.

Meanwhile, I had already become well acquainted with the two foremost archers and sportsmen in that area of Tennessee: Edward McNish and his brother Tom. When I asked them if they wanted to go, they were most eager and agreed immediately.

My friend from the Tennessee Wildlife Association was as good as his word; and on the morning of December 26, the three of us with homemade osage orange bows and birch hunting arrows rode out from Tellico Plains into the Unaka Mountains with our guide Ben Ellis and three of his trusty Plott hounds. These hounds were descendants of hounds bred in Germany for boar hunting centuries ago.

To start the hunt of the "chase" type, the guide goes to a likely area, locates tracks of the wild boar, and when he finds tracks or signs fresh enough he puts the dogs on the trail. They keep on the trail until the boar is located and flushed from his bed (which is in dense underbrush). Then the "chase," or "race" as many of the natives call it, begins. The guide knows when the dogs have jumped a boar by the change in the quality of the barking and its increased tempo. The guides and hunters must increase

Fig. 10–2. Ben Ellis, veteran guide on Russian boar hunts, and one of his dogs observe a pine tree cut by boar tusks. (Tenn. Conservation Dept. photo.)

their tempo also if they are to be successful. They must manage to get within good shooting range of the boar at a time when the dogs have temporarily brought the boar to "bay." The dogs may bring the boar to bay many times; and the boar may break bay and move on many times before the guide and hunters are able to arrive and shoot the boar, if at all. After the "race" has started, the really tough part of the hunt is keeping up with the guide, climbing hills, plunging down through ravines, wading rough rock-bottom streams, tearing through endless lengths of green briars—and all the time your lungs are splitting and you wonder how long you can take it.

This was the way it was on the day the first wild boar was taken with bow and arrow. The "race," however, did not start until eleven o'clock in the morning when we already were bone-tired from keeping up with the guide, trudging through rain, wind, and occasional sleet. However, the changed tempo of the baying dogs and the guide's quick response, "They've flushed a boar," sparked the needed energy; and we promptly forgot our fatigue as we raced after the barking dogs. The race this first time was a short one. The boar was brought to bay at the edge of the Tellico River. Arriving a little ahead of the other two hunters, my arrow was first to reach the mark and to bag the boar (Fig. 10–3).

When it was all over, I confess I was disappointed that this first boar shot in America was not bigger and fiercer. But there were other days to come. I honestly feel that Ben Ellis, our guide (although he never said so

Fig. 10–3. Dr. Harlan G. Metcalf and the first Russian wild boar shot with bow and arrow in the States. The boar was taken in the Cherokee National Forest in Tennessee in 1938. (Tenn. Conservation Dept. photo.)

to us), purposely kept us away from the stamping grounds of any big boar that first day since he was not really convinced as to the killing power of a hunting arrow. After seeing my arrow strike home the first day (December 26, 1938), he was convinced. He also felt that we had the necessary stamina for the chase.

A SECOND BOAR IS BAGGED. On the next day (December 27, 1938), the guides took the two McNish brothers, Ed and Tom, and a photographer into an area that he knew was dominated by a really big boar. The boar was soon flushed by the dogs. They brought him to bay five or six different times. Each time he broke away before the guides and archers arrived. When the hunters finally reached the boar at bay, he charged Ed McNish from a thicket before Ed could even draw his arrow. Ed vaulted out of its path and into a clump of briars, barely escaping the boar as it rushed past. Twice the boar treed the photographer and guides. The three dogs then brought the boar to bay again. The infuriated boar charged the dogs, one of which the boar picked up and threw against a tree 10 feet away, severely ripping the dog's hindquarter. A lucky shot from a 32-caliber hand gun of the guide severed a tendon in one of the rear legs of the boar. It then charged Tom McNish, but Tom's arrow met it head on between the eye and the ear. The arrow penetrated the skull and severed the spinal cord in the neck. The 320-lb. wild boar was dead (Fig. 10–4).

The sport of hunting wild boar with bow and arrow was thus launched. Mr. Val Solyom, Game Technician for the Tennessee State Conservation Department, commented that it had not yet been established that mature wild boars could be taken by archers without an assist from firearms.

MORE HUNTS IN THE FALL OF 1939. In the fall of 1939, sixteen eager archers registered to hunt wild boar, four of which were successful.

I shall describe briefly some incidents from two of the successful hunts with bow and arrow, which emphasize three things: the skill of the guides in handling their dogs, the toughness of the wild boar's protective shield, and precautions archers should take if they contemplate hunting boar with bow and arrow.

On Thanksgiving Day, 1939, Val Solyom, who had become interested in bowhunting; Dr. Darwin A. Hindman, Dean of Men at the University of Missouri, Columbia, Missouri (former collegemate); and I left the Tellico Plains Hotel for the hunt. Val decided to try still-hunting and see if he could stalk some wild boar close enough for a shot. He left his car with Dr. Hindman and me. We stopped for our guide, Ben Ellis, and three of his fine hounds and then drove to a section drained by the Upper Bald River.

The dogs were put on a trail and within a half-hour had flushed a boar and the "race" was on. I have played all sports but never have engaged

Fig. 10-4. Russian boar bagged by archers Ed and Tom McNish in Tennessee's Cherokee National Forest. On the left are guides Zeke and Ben Ellis. (Tenn. Conservation Dept. photo.)

in any that taxed my heart and lungs so continually as did hunting wild boar with the bow. Ten or eleven times the guide reported that the dogs had the boar at bay, but before we could reach the spot the boar had fought off the dogs and moved on.

Finally, on a high ridge of the Unaka Mountains, the guide stopped. We assumed it was for a rest, so we flopped on the ground to get it while we could. The guide did not stop to rest, but to ponder a problem. He said the boar and dogs had crossed the state line and were now in North Carolina. He wondered whether we should follow into North Carolina or not. He said he had a North Carolina license and asked if we did. We did not. Then after a moment of intent listening, the guide said, "Good, the dogs have turned the boar. He's headed back into Tennessee. He's in Tennessee." Then the guide called us to him and pointed in the direction in which we could just hear the dogs baying. He said, "Do you see this great valley?" "Yes," we said. Then the guide spoke again, "Do you see that high hill on the other side of the valley? . . . The boar is at bay on the far side of that hill." The guide stood still waiting. We asked him what he was waiting for. He indicated that he was not sure we wanted to continue. He was used to guiding gun hunters who wanted guides to bring the boar to them in range to shoot. We said, "Let's go; that's why we are here." So he plunged down the hill with us at his heels. We made the best time we could, hoping the boar would still be at bay when we arrived. We sloshed across the stream and swamp at the bottom and started climbing the hill. My longer legs gave me an advantage, and I pushed ahead in the direction of the barking dogs. As I came to the top of the hill, I began to wonder whether I would have breath and strength enough to draw the arrow back when I finally reached the boar. The excited barking grew louder and louder. Soon I saw the dogs: one in the middle facing straight away from me and the other two facing inwards one on each side. I walked cautiously then with bow and arrow ready. When I had reached a spot about 12 yards from the first or middle dog, I saw the boar in the midst of a rhododendron thicket. I could see a black area of his neck about 4 or 5 inches in diameter. This spot I had to hit, so I drew the arrow back to the anchor. I did not shoot then, however, because directly below the black target was the middle dog. If my arrow was short, he might be hit. Just then the guide who had come up behind me sensed the situation and made a peculiar whistle. Instantly the dog that was in my line of fire crouched down and pulled himself back away from the boar. Now I had at least 3 feet leeway below the boar's neck. So I again drew the arrow back and shot. The arrow hit where aimed. The boar made one leap about 3 feet into the air, shook all over momentarily, and dropped dead. The arrow penetrated the cervical vertebrae of the neck and severed the spinal cord. Death was instantaneous.

This instance was described to show the skill with which the guide handled his dogs and his close communication with them at all times.

Another instance of the guide's resourcefulness was shown when, discovering no one in the party had rope to tie the boar to a pole, he disappeared and came back with two green hickory withes he had cut and twisted back and forth to make them pliable. These he used as rope to tie the boar's feet to the pole.

This boar was nearly 200 pounds in weight; was mature; and had sharp, well-developed tusks. One of the dogs had been "tusked" once but was not seriously injured. It was lucky that the arrow hit the neck and cord as this boar's shield of tough gristle was at least an inch thick. We carried the boar downhill to the little stream that turned out to be the head waters of the Bald River. Although the stream was wet and rocky, it still offered the best walking back to the car 6 miles away.

DR. HINDMAN'S TURN. We slept well at Tellico Plains that night and arrived at the guide's house early in the morning in Val Solyom's car where we picked up Ben Ellis (the guide), his 14-year-old boy who wanted to see bows and arrows shot, and three big hounds. We soon arrived at a place that looked good to Ben. While Dr. Hindman and I busied ourselves sharpening his arrows with a file and adjusting his quiver. Ben unleashed his dogs to scout for boar signs. Ben's boy said he would wander down the road a bit. Dr. Hindman said to me, "Gold, how many arrows are you taking?" I said I would take only four arrows just to play safe because after all this was his day to get a boar. Hindman said, "Well, I'll take six arrows." This was really ridiculous. Both of us should have taken at least a dozen arrows apiece and we had them in the car.

Five minutes later Ben's boy ran back to us all excited and told his dad that a big boar had just crossed the road about 100 yards from where we were. Ben immediately fired one shot from his 32-caliber hand gun, which called all the dogs back to him. Ben and the boy placed the dogs on the trail, and Hindman followed close behind them. By the time I hurriedly strapped on my quiver and strung my bow and got to the road, the rest were out of sight. It was no trick to follow them as the dogs were barking loudly and had already brought the boar to bay. I stepped off the road into the woods in the direction of the barking. I first noted Ben's boy sitting in a tree 6 to 8 feet above the ground 10 yards farther on; Ben Ellis was perched in the only other tree nearby. Moving slowly on I saw a very large boar with the three dogs at points around it. Off to the left about 8 yards was Hindman with bow drawn back ready to shoot. There was no tree near me so I froze and watched with an arrow on my string. Although Hindman's first arrow barely missed the boar, it helped to establish the range; and his second arrow hit in the middle of the boar's thorax. In the wild excitement that followed, both Hindman and I shot and scored hits. About this time Hindman appeared suddenly at my side and said quickly, "Gold, got any more arrows?" I said, "Here's one; it's all I have left. Make it good." He stalked back and sped our last arrow into the boar's chest. The boar responded by charging one of the dogs. The guide in the tree, fearing his dog would be killed, shifted his position to get his 32-caliber hand gun. The boar seeing the movement charged to the base of the guide's tree, looking up at him. I yelled to the guide not to use his gun, saying that the boar would soon drop. The guide replied, "You don't know these boar like I do." And of course I didn't. Meanwhile, Hindman, without arrows, had spotted a small tree back up the hill about 25 yards away. He started inching his way up the hill to reach it, but the boar spotted Hindman moving and immediately charged him. The guide fired two shots at the boar. Hindman reached the tree just a second ahead of the boar and started climbing for safety. The boar, however, caught Hindman's left leg against the tree with one of his tusks, slashing a 6-inch gash through the outside of the thick leather hunting boot, two pairs of woolen socks, and the skin over the ankle and outer leg.

The boar then rolled over dead. It would have died from any one of the arrows that penetrated the thorax and into the lungs. The arrows had difficulty piercing the 1½- to 2-inch shield over the heart and lungs, but two had pierced both lungs and lodged into the far thoracic wall (Fig. 10–5). The entire period of the wild excitement had lasted only a few moments.

This boar weighed over 400 lbs. When it was skinned, two 32-caliber bullets were found; one in the skin since it did not get through and one

Fig. 10–5. Dr. D. A. Hindman, Professor of Physical Education, University of Missouri, and his 400-lb. wild boar shot with bow and arrow in Tennessee in 1939. (Tenn. Conservation Dept. photo.)

just barely beneath the skin outside the subcutaneous tissue. This was proof that only the arrows killed the boar.

The other two archers to kill wild boar that same fall of 1939 were Mrs. Edward McNish and Mr. Buck Allison (Figs. 14–19 and 10–6).

Fig. 10–6. The McNish camp on Bald River, Tennessee. Buck Allison and Mrs. Ed McNish warm themselves by the campfire as they discuss their luck in bagging the two wild boars strung up. Guide Zeke Ellis is busy with the dogs. (Tenn. Conservation Dept. photo.)

PRECAUTIONS IN EUROPEAN BOAR HUNTING. Some of the points on which all archers agreed as a result of these wild boar hunts were:

1. Each archer should always carry at least 1 dozen arrows in his quiver and another dozen in his car.
2. Each archer should have with him two extra bowstrings. Bowstrings are easily frayed and eventually broken by constant contact with green or saw briars.
3. The drawing weight of the bow used should be as great as one can control. My bow was a 75-lb. osage orange bow. A 60-lb. glass laminated bow is the recommended minimum weight. This heavy weight is essential in driving an arrow through the boar's shield.
4. The broadheads of the hunting arrows should be barbless so that they will

be easy to withdraw from the quiver. The arrows used should weigh at least 1 ounce and preferably 500 grains.

5. If close enough to be sure of it, a neck shot is satisfactory since large blood vessels as well as the spinal cord are possible targets. Such a shot avoids the thick, tough shield. A diagonal shot from the side and a little to the rear and ranging forward into the lungs and heart will avoid the shield.

6. The importance of being physically fit for climbing hills and agility for climbing trees cannot be stressed too highly.

MAJOR REFERENCES FOR HUNTING WILD BOAR IN THE UNITED STATES.
It is still posible for archers to hunt wild boar with bow and arrow in either the Santeetla National Forest in North Carolina or the Cherokee National Forest of Tennessee.* However, the rules for such hunts and the dates may change from year to year. Therefore, if archers desire to hunt wild boar in Tennessee, they should write to the Tennessee Game and Fish Commission, Nashville, Tennessee. If interested in hunting wild boar in North Carolina, they should contact the North Carolina Wildlife Resources Commission, Raleigh, North Carolina.

HUNTING THE JAVELINA (PECCARY)

The javelina is a 3-foot long, 45- to 50-lb. piglike animal that lives along the Mexican border; namely, in southwestern Texas, southeastern New Mexico, and southern Arizona. Its appearance is a lot like that of the "piney woods rooters" (feral pigs) of the Southeast. Its head appears overly large in comparison to the rest of the body. In other respects, however, the javelina is a miniature in comparison to the much larger feral pig. Its appearance as it raises its bristles on end and chatters its teeth in anger commands respect from most hunters (Fig. 10–7).

Javelinas commonly are found on the higher mesas and in the rocky canyons of the foothills and mountainsides within their range. The rimrock and caves along the main and side (feeder) canyons, as well as the dense tangle of cacti and brush of the canyon floors, provide cover for loafing and escape. In general, the animals feed mainly early and late in the day and then lie quiet during the heat of the day. In the winter season, however, they may feed at any hour of the day.

Hunting the javelina is a sporting venture. In Arizona, the principal method of hunting is by stalking, with the open season usually being set for 2 weeks in February. Texas has a season for javelinas in October in some counties. A few counties are open to hunting all year round; some others have a continuous closed season.

* A couple of excellent works on European boar in the United States are: Leroy C. Stegeman, "The European Wild Boar in the Cherokee National Forest, Tennessee," *Journal of Mammalogy,* XIX, No. 3 (1938) , 279–90; Perry Jones, *European Wild Boar in North Carolina* (Raleigh, N.C.: North Carolina Wildlife Resources Commission, 1959).

Fig. 10–7. A javelina is a worthy trophy for any bowhunter. This one was bagged by Dr. F. H. Kenagy, pioneer bowhunter from Washington and formerly of Idaho. (Photograph courtesy of Dr. F. H. Kenagy.)

To the bowhunter stalking for javelinas, the biggest task is to locate the whereabouts of the critters, which are not easily found. One must first be able to find the general locality where a herd is active. This will require being able to read field signs left by the javelinas, such as tracks, rootings, or fecal dropping sites.

Tracks may be found in sandy areas in arroyos where the herd has crossed or in soft soil. Their tracks differ from those of deer in being shorter and rounder at the front edge.

Rootings, if fresh, are a good indication of current presence. They may also indicate feeding habits of the animals at the time, thereby suggesting other areas to check. Prickly-pear pads and fruits are among the chief foods.

Areas where fecal droppings are concentrated provide good indication of presence. However, be sure to check to make certain the droppings are fresh. If all the droppings are old, the herd may have moved on to another area.

Once the general area of an active herd has been located, the hunter then needs to spy to find the animals themselves. For this purpose, binoculars are very useful. The hunter should climb to a vantage point in the area, arriving there early in the morning. He should perch himself comfortably on a prominence and use his binoculars to search the surrounding countryside for javelinas. An extra-thorough job of scanning the area will pay dividends. If javelinas are located, the job of stalking has just begun.

To approach to within shooting distance, the hunter must give consideration to the animals' good sense of smell and hearing. Its eyesight, however, is not very good, especially if the hunter remains motionless. Depending on the direction of the wind and the lay of the land, the hunter may now need to circle the herd and approach it from the other (downwind) side. Patience and extreme caution in the approach at close quarters is essential. Search every bit of cover as you approach, looking for "parts" of the animals as they remain screened and partly hidden by the surrounding cover. Move ahead only when you are certain you have thoroughly scanned the cover. When you get near and downwind from the herd, you may be able to smell it.

When your opportunity for a shot comes, you had better take it without delay as javelinas have a way of disappearing in a flash. As in the case with larger-game species, a diagonal hit into the chest cavity, when available, is to be preferred.

Archers preferring to hunt as a party may cooperate in hunting a canyon in which a herd is known to be located. In such a case, one or more bowmen may sneak up the ridges bordering the canyon floor so as not to spook any javelinas in the area. The strategy is for the hunters to station themselves at places along the rimrocks where the animals might try to escape if spooked from areas below. After a previously agreed upon lapse of time, the remaining two or three hunters slowly stalk up the canyon. As they proceed, they search for dark-looking objects, which may be javelinas feeding, loafing, or on the move to escape.

At times, an animal or two may have taken cover in a rock cave, especially later in the day. A javelina hiding in such a place can usually be made to betray its presence if the hunter will pitch a few rocks into the dark cavity. Any animal present will respond by chattering its teeth. Such an animal though irritated is not as dangerous an adversary as is commonly portrayed by many hunters. By repeated goading by pitching rocks at it, such an animal may eventually be brought out of the cave. The emerging animal may appear as if it "exploded" from its hiding place. A wise bowhunter will be prepared for a quick shot as the animal charges out. While such an animal may appear to be charging the hunter on some occasions, yet in all likelihood, it is just trying to get out of the hostile area and merely happens to run in the direction of the hunter. Nevertheless, its 1- to 3-inch sharp-edged tusks can be severe weapons if the hunter happens to be in the way of its flight.

If the javelina is hit and downed, it is well to be absolutely certain it is dead before the hunter stoops to examine his fallen quarry.

From mid-morning until late afternoon, when javelinas normally have taken cover, a lone bowhunter may find it advantageous to slowly stalk along canyon edges and the edges of washes and saddles to search out the quarry to close enough quarters to secure a favorable shot.

Once your javelina has been bagged, a careful job of cleaning will insure good meat. Barbecued javelina is delicious eating.

Javelinas have a scent gland on their rump, just above the tail, that emits a pungent odor when the animal becomes excited. Care must be taken so that no trace of secretion from the gland comes in contact with the flesh while dressing an animal. If it does, it will taint the meat. Old-timers claim that this gland, as well as the testicles of the boars, must be removed as soon as possible after the animal is recovered. It is claimed that leaving these parts on for any length of time will spoil the meat for eating. As with the deer, this practice seems to be based more on belief and custom than on fact. By leaving the gland on, you will have an intact skin, which makes excellent leather when tanned.

If your ambition includes a hunt for javelinas, be sure to contact the Game Department of the state of your choice for hunting. Write for necessary information on seasons and other regulations. A local archer can be of considerable help in selecting a choice area for hunting.

HUNTING WILD HOGS

Some of the southeastern states, notably South Carolina, Georgia, Florida, Alabama, Mississippi, Louisiana, and Arkansas have feral hogs, hogs of domestic origin that have lived in the wild for several generations. Some are as wild as deer. They are lean and "rangy" looking, and many sport long "razor-sharp" tusks. Locally these hogs commonly are referred to as piney woods rooters, or just plain wild hogs.

Over the years, these critters have provided much sport. Their popularity in Louisiana has resulted in the development of a special hunting dog, the "Catahoula hog dog."

The principal method of hunting wild hogs consists of running the critters with dogs. The huntsmen do their shooting from stands selected along paths or in brushy areas where the hogs are likely to run. These piney woods rooters are both smart and hardy. If brought to bay by dogs and approached too closely by a hunter, they can become mean customers. They may break the stalemate of being held at bay with a charge that will send any self-respecting hunter scurrying for safety up a tree.

A good bow with at least a 50-lb. pull and a razor-sharp broadhead are recommended. Where choice is available, arrows weighing at least an ounce seem advisable. Last but not least, try for a diagonal hit, driving the arrow forward into the chest cavity. Such a hit may save you the trouble of scrambling up a tree to avoid an onrushing and very angry hog. Such a hit will drop your animal more quickly.

11

Small-Game Hunting

Bowhunters are fortunate in that small-game hunting is available near almost every community in the country. To the average city dweller, and farm lad, the cottontail leads the list as fair game. Not far behind follow the fox squirrel and/or gray squirrel. Each of the three species contribute considerably to the sport of hunting with bow and arrow. Information on hunting these sporting game species follows.

HUNTING THE COTTONTAIL

The cottontail rabbit is the number one game animal of the neophyte hunter. An estimated fifty million are harvested each year, mostly by gun hunters. Cottontails are found on farmland, woodland, wasteland, and in cities—seemingly in all types of habitat where cover is available.

Cottontails like other game species and farm crops produce an annual increase that is available for harvest. In the case of the cottontail, the population each fall consists of about three-fourths young of the year. Accordingly, there is an annual "turnover" (destruction) of three-fourths of the population. The annual increase is the surplus for which hunters and nature compete for a share. Predators, disease, parasites, and highway mortality are the hunters' chief competitors.

To the father who wishes to teach sportsmanship and hunting safety to his teenager, the cottontail is a favorite game species (Fig. 11–1). It is an elusive target as it bounds and zigzags along in its dash to escape. Then too, the usual abundance of rabbits provides frequent opportunities for a fair shot, a condition that adds greatly to the attractiveness of the sport.

Knowing the habits of the cottontail is important for productive hunting. This is especially true where the hunting is done without the use of dogs to trail the rabbits.

Daily habits of cottontails are influenced by temperatures. In the Lake States region of the United States, cottontails usually spend their resting periods in burrows underground when temperatures fall below 20° F. but rest in grassy or other cover above ground in warmer temperatures. In some other northern areas, they may hole up at slightly higher temperatures.

The type and arrangement of available cover may also affect the cotton-

127

Fig. 11–1. When Chris Haugen took his first cottontail, there was cause for celebrating. He had learned hunting the "hard way."

tail and its population. These animals normally provide the bulk of the diet of foxes and great horned owls. Since it is handicapped in having no adequate weapon for defense, its survival depends on staying close to escape cover. For this reason, it is seldom that a cottontail strays as much as 100 yards from escape cover. The bunny that lives to a ripe old age (2 or 3 years) is the one that is wise enough to stay within a few hops of cover where he can escape from most of his enemies.

A variety of tackle is used for cottontail hunting. Some favor blunt arrows; others use broadheads. Target or field arrows if tipped with rubber blunt heads are adequate for small-game hunting, but regular target and field points are not suitable. With blunts, it is recommended that a bow with at least 35 lbs. of pull be used so as to provide adequate striking power. With broadhead arrows properly sharpened, bows as light as 25 lbs. may be used if they have good cast.

Cottontail hunting in the Midwest corn areas is most productive around areas with brushy cover, along the edge of farm woodlots, or in the farm windbreaks around buildings. Some veteran bowhunting friends in northern Iowa have hunted such farm groves with success for years (Fig. 11–2). The bunnies are usually abundant in such groves; both food and cover are available.

While waiting for a fresh tracking snow, secure permission from the farmer on whose land you wish to hunt.

Fig. 11–2. Cottontails provide excellent sport for bowmen. These lucky archers who hunted near Joice, Iowa, one cold and snowy winter day in 1961 are Archie Bilyeu, Floyd Thomas, Ray Wogen, and A. O. Haugen, all of Iowa.

Before the hunt starts, it is well to take into consideration the permanent-type cover for which the rabbits are sure to dash when disturbed. Such cover may consist of brush piles, trash piles, burrows, and buildings under which they may hide. Proper strategy calls for first placing an archer near each type of escape cover where he can get a clear shot at any rabbit that scrambles for cover. The remaining archers then stalk through the grove, proceeding cautiously while looking for cottontails sitting crouched in their "form." These forms, or beds as they are commonly called in many areas, are places where the rabbits sit in hiding during the daytime. Such sitting places are usually located in a clump of grass or weeds, under a leaning cornstalk, or similar cover. A smart hunter carefully scans the cover ahead as he stalks on and learns to spot a cottontail even though it may be almost completely hidden as it crouches motionless in its form.

With good tracking conditions, the bowman can trail his rabbit, carefully watching to locate where the tracks end. That is where the rabbit is hidden. In many cases, the cottontail has his form 25 to 50 yards out in open fields adjoining woody cover. In such a situation, even an elevated piece of sod in a plowed field may be the hiding place.

In times when deep drifts of snow pile up along roadsides or near woody borders, cottontails often make shallow cavities in the snowbanks where they may be spotted from close quarters. Hunting along such drifts may help put rabbit meat on the table. Fried rabbit, in case you have not tried it, is as delicious as chicken.

If you have a couple of good beagle hounds for hunting, you are a fortunate bowhunter. With such hounds you are equipped to hunt extensive areas such as meadows or forest areas. The strategy consists of jumping the rabbit and letting the beagles chase it in hope that the rabbit's circling or running before the hounds may present opportunities for a fleeting shot. Beagles in their slow trailing generally keep the rabbit moving but do not run fast enough to force it to take cover in a burrow.

HUNTING SQUIRRELS

Hunting tree squirrels with bow and arrow is not as difficult as it may appear. They present a small target; but with proper care in stalking, they can be approached to within 10 yards.

The most important element for success is to dress in camouflage clothing and to stalk with patience. Such clothing seems to completely confuse squirrels if sudden movements are avoided.

Blunt arrows with flu flu fletching are considered most appropriate for shooting at squirrels overhead. If on the ground, any kind of arrow will do.

At feeding hours (early and late in the day) when squirrels are most likely to move around on the ground, they can be "waited out" by standing motionless for 20 minutes to a half-hour. Select what appears to be a good feeding area, a place with a good crop of acorns or nuts, or a woodlot or row of trees adjoining a cornfield. Check the ground for signs of a worn path from the cornfield to the nearest tree, then to and past the bases of other trees. Fresh claw marks (scratches) on the tree trunk are an indication of extent of use.

When such signs of use are found, take a stand with your shoulder or back against a tree trunk. Stand as still as a stone figure. If you approach quietly and stand still, the squirrels usually will resume feeding before long. Wait until you get the squirrel in the best possible spot for a clean shot. There is no need to hurry. So long as you think there is a chance that the position for the shot can be improved, wait.

If the animal is feeding in a woodlot where brush may interfere with a clean shot, watch the squirrel carefully and stalk it. Each time its head roots deep in the leaves for another acorn or seed, take one more step forward. By this technique, you can get closer, a step at a time, to gain a favorable shooting position. A successful stalk may require 10 minutes or more, but a successful shot will be worth it.

When you have reached the proper position for shooting, draw your bow at a time when the squirrel is temporarily distracted by something else. When you do draw, do so slowly and with continuous motion.

If the animal is missed and it climbs high in a tree, you have a much more difficult shot. In such a position, the use of flu flu blunts is most advantageous because a miss that strikes a limb will allow the arrow to glance or bounce off and fall back to earth nearby. If a blunt strikes and dumps the squirrel to the ground, go to it quickly and make certain it does not recover from what may have been a glancing blow.

Do not forget that squirrels in addition to being sporting game animals are delicious eating (Fig. 11–3). Good luck and good squirrel hunting.

Fig. 11–3. While the fun is in the hunt, admiration is acceptable even in the ranks of the juniors. This Alabama gray squirrel was a trophy as well as meat on the table.

III

HISTORY OF ARCHERY

12

Primitive Archery

The history of development of weapons by prehistoric people is hidden in the dim past, yet occasional clues to early development still are being unearthed from time to time. Archaeologists will yet add substantially to known history of aborigine weapons. This is especially so now that science, through the use of radioactive carbon dating techniques, has made it possible to place reasonably accurate dates on artifacts.

The chronology of development of weapons probably started with a stick or stone with which to strike small animals over the head. Next in order there probably followed a sharpened stick and hand-wielded spears. The bola, consisting of three hide-wrapped stones connected by thongs and which was hurled at animals' legs to entangle them in the strands, is known to date back at least 400,000 years in Africa. Weapons with striking power from a distance must have followed; namely, the sling for heaving rocks, the atlatl for throwing spears, the blowgun, and the bow.

Information on the earliest use of the bow and arrow has been unearthed by archaeologists. These scientists report that the first to use arrows with flint-tipped heads was the Aurignacian race of men who lived in southern France at least 25,000 years ago. Arrows with mere sharpened points, or with bone tips, preceded the chipped stone points. These were Paleolithic times with stone-age men. Their chipped points and other stone implements were of rough-flaked type as these early-day cave dwellers had not yet learned to polish or grind stone to smooth shapes.

Chipped stone heads were extensively used on the tip of both spears and arrows. The effectiveness of such heads is attested by the fact that early inhabitants of the Old World lived mostly by means of a hunting economy for thousands of generations. A sample of stone arrowheads used by aborigines in the state of Alabama are shown in Fig. 12–2.

The interest of prehistoric men in hunting is recorded on the walls of caves once occupied by these ancient hunters in western North America, southern France, and Spain. Surprisingly, the cave art in Europe, which is one of the great artistic archievements of all time, has survived down through at least 25,000 years of time.

How these ancient archers practiced so that they might be successful at bringing home game for food is unknown. One thing is fairly certain;

they needed to take game frequently or kill numbers of animals at certain seasons and then dry the meat to preserve it as the Indians did in the Americas in historic times. In either case, reasonable accuracy in shooting their bows must have been of considerable value for their survival (Fig. 12–1). Perhaps roving as a form of archery practice for hunting had its origin back that early in time. In a sense, it would seem that roving in its original form consisted of shooting at casual marks in the woods and meadows.

Fig. 12–1. Once upon a time odds were even for the hunter and the hunted —bare skin or bear skin. (Courtesy of O. Warbach.)

In the beginning, all archery was "field archery" of a sort. The bow was a weapon of the hunt and for attacking or defense against enemies. It is probable that it had not yet been adapted for use for organized games. Still there probably existed keen competition for the honor of being the first hunter in the family or clan to down his game. Archery in the beginning, and up through the 250 centuries since that time, was no doubt an art of instinctive shooting. How could it be otherwise in a food-gathering and hunting economy where no standard unit of measurement existed and where time meant little except time for hunting to provide food for the family or camp?

EARLY ARCHERY IN THE NEW WORLD

There is evidence that archery entered the New World by way of a land bridge that once connected the North American continent with Asia in the Alaska area. Toward the end of the last great glacial period when the land bridge disappeared, probably a little less than 20,000 years ago, primitive people from northeastern Asia crossed to the American continent. These people eventually became the American Indian. For about a thousand generations, these Indians fed and defended themselves primarily through the use of the spear, the spear-throwing atlatl, and bow. Their missiles though tipped with bone or blades of stone were effective for both hunting and war (Fig. 12–2).

Not one, but several invasions by Asiatic people are believed to have occurred. Some of these people who lived primarily as hunters until about

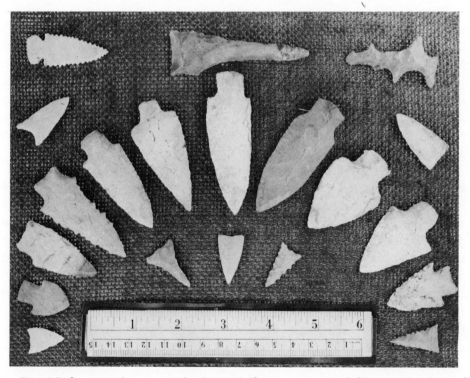

Fig. 12–2. Missiles to suit the hunter's fancy were available even in the red man's day. Indians roaming the area now known as North Alabama left these artifacts, including arrow and spear heads, drills, and an erratic (*bottom right*).

the year A.D. 1 left artifacts now referred to as Folsom and Cochise cultures. Even the Indians of the highest culture, such as the Mayan, Aztecs, and Incas, existed on a hunting economy until about that time.

Some American anthropologists believe the New World man probably brought with him from Asia only a simple unbacked bow, and arrows fletched with two whole feathers. This being the case, some New World aborigines may be credited with probably having developed for themselves the principles of improving bows by gluing a thin layer of sinew to the back and belly, and with having invented for themselves the principle of using three split feathers for fletching arrows. Some Eskimos strengthened their bows by tying cords of sinew to the back side so that the sinew was stretched like an elastic cord when the bow was pulled to full draw.

Early weapons on the American continent included the spear-throwing atlatl as well as the bow. The term "atlatl" is an Aztec word for the spear-throwing stick that was once used throughout the Americas as a weapon of the early inhabitants. Some think its extensive use preceded the bow.

At the time the white man came to the Americas, the atlatl was principally limited to the most civilized regions; namely, Middle America and Peru, where agriculture largely had replaced hunting as a way of life. Wilder tribes still dependent on hunting for a living relied mainly on the bow because of its greater accuracy.

Specimens of spears recovered from dry caves of the Southwest indicate a length of about 5 feet and a diameter of about ⅜ to ½ inch. The throwing stick, some of which were about 2 feet long, was so designed that one end engaged the rear end of the spear. Such a stick produced the effect of a longer throwing arm and made it possible to exert additional force to the spear over a longer distance. Stone weights at times were added to atlatls to add throwing force to the stick.

An archaeologist by the name of Brown made tests of the relative accuracy and striking power of rough-made specimens of arrows shot from a 60-lb. osage orange wood bow and a 60-inch spear thrown with an atlatl. He made the spear barreled in shape, ½ inch in diameter at the middle and ⅜ inch at the ends. He tested the accuracy of each by aiming at a 4-foot target at 30 yards. Hits were scored with thirty-one out of thirty-six shots with the bow, and six out of thirty-six with spear and atlatl. This does not seem like much accuracy to a seasoned archer. Brown, however, made the equipment that he thought an aborigine might have made for himself— equipment that obviously is far inferior to present-day equipment.

When compared for striking distance, the arrow was shot a maximum of 137 yards; whereas, the maximum distance for the spear and atlatl totaled only 81 yards. Again this seems like mediocre performance.

When tipped with modern steel broadheads and compared for striking power, both weapons showed about the same degree of penetration in a piece of board. These comparisons indicate greater degree of accuracy and longer striking distance for arrows. Results also bear out that at close quarters where accuracy is not so important, spears and atlatls also were deadly weapons.

Today the atlatl and spear are still in use by some Aztec Indians in Mexico and some Nunivac Eskimos of western Alaska. Its use now seems mostly limited to hunting for birds. The multipronged spears utilized are hurled into flocks of waterbirds after a close approach by canoe.

The striking power of some of the American aborigine's bows was illustrated by a captive Apalachi Indian of the Florida area who amazed onlooking Spaniards in 1539 by driving an arrow through a suit of the Spaniard's fancy and much cherished armor. De Soto's men received a painful "taste" of the effectiveness of the bow and arrow when they clashed with Chief Tascalusa and his warriors in southern Alabama. All of De Soto's men (between 600 and 700) except the Holy padres were wounded, some with several arrows. Although De Soto won the battle, his losses of materials and horses were of such a serious nature that his expedition never fully recovered from the attack.

If De Soto had been without horses, his expedition would probably have come to an early end at the hands of the redskins. While a Spaniard fired a single shot and made ready for another, each Indian reportedly shot six or seven arrows. This provided the Indians with an edge in firepower.

Many a pioneer learned firsthand the effectiveness of the bow as a weapon at close quarters. For accuracy and striking power at a distance, however, the pioneer's muzzle loader was a superior weapon, although very slow in firepower. Even the Indian saw the superior qualities of firearms for hunting and quickly adopted the white man's weapon. With improved muzzle loaders in their possession, some of the more fortunate tribes found that they could defeat neighboring enemies of long standing.

With the westward roll of settlers and the subjugation and/or annihilation of the free-roving Indian population in America, the bow dropped out of sight as a weapon for hunting and/or warfare. Its use had not yet gained a following for recreational purposes in America.

And so we come to the end of the use of the bow and arrow as a weapon for war so far as civilized parts of the world are concerned. On the target range and on the field courses, archery now is the basis for one of our most highly regarded sports. As a weapon of the hunt, the bow has found a "new" use—for sport instead of for bringing home daily meat for the pot.

Archery in the western states seems to have been influenced considerably by W. J. "Chief" Compton, a man whose stature has grown almost to that of a patron saint to field and hunting archery. Compton's archery in turn stemmed from his association with Sioux Indians who had adopted him as a boy, and from whom he had attained his priceless store of hunting lore.

Western archery, accordingly, seems to have had some of its origin from Indian sources. This may at least partly explain why westerners were almost solidly in favor of bare-bow (instinctive) type shooting during the early days of field archery.

Artificial means of sighting seems to have been ingrained in eastern archery from the beginning, probably stemming from the successes and writings of Horace Ford, an Englishman who adopted the point of aim in breaking all previous records.

Archery offers a significant lesson in life. A Chinese philosopher focused our attention on that lesson when he reportedly wrote: "The Master said, in archery we are given an insight into the way of the wise. When an archer misses the center of the target, he turns around and seeks for the cause of the failure in himself."

13

Field Archery
Becomes Organized

A NATIONAL FIELD ARCHERY ORGANIZATION IS BORN

In considering early history of the organization of the National Field Archery Association (N.F.A.A.), a record of the trials and tribulations of individuals and groups that helped further this form of archery is of interest.

In the beginning there were only isolated individuals or hunting pals who expressed an interest in informal or roving-type shooting. They were "lone wolves" in their sport. Interest, however, grew and soon attracted many able men who took an active part in organizational affairs. Men of real vision came forward to provide the much-needed leadership to promote and organize the National Field Archery Association. The continued help of these leaders soon directed the young association to success and worldwide recognition. This fact bears witness to the unselfish contributions of pioneer field and hunting archers.

There is little need here to present details of the impetus given hunting archery following the Civil War by Will and Maurice Thompson, a couple of Georgians. However, if their articles and book, titled *Witchery of Archery,* had appeared at a time when big-game animals were more numerous, the impact would no doubt have been immediate. As it was, their articles on hunting archery appeared at a time when deer populations were at their lowest ebb in America. The great slaughter of big-game animals and the destruction of their habitat had taken its toll until deer and other big-game species had become extinct or nearly so in many states.

It remained for publications of Art Young and Dr. Saxton Pope to set the stage for modern-day expansion of archery. Their exploits with bow and arrow came at a time when deer populations again were increasing and expanding into suitable areas. Accounts of their hunts with William "Chief" Compton shortly following World War I sparked an immediate response from sports-minded individuals. Those whose interest in formal target archery had waned or whose original interest in archery centered on informal roving or hunting were among the first to join the ranks of the bowhunter clan.

The advent of *Ye Sylvan Archer* in the spring of 1927 was a landmark for bowhunting and field-type archery. It was a new and delightful archery magazine devoted mostly to the less formal types of hunting and field archery. Its originators, B. G. Thompson and J. E. Davis, were professors at Oregon State College at Corvalis. Davis became the long-time editor of the magazine but with other editors filling in for short periods. Both men had a genuine interest in field-type shooting.

The magazine, first intended for western archers with an interest in the less-formal types of archery, was destined to grow to great importance to archers everywhere. In 1929 it became the official organ of the newly founded Western Archery Association. Even greater recognition was to come when later it became the official magazine for the N.F.A.A.

Early issues of *Ye Sylvan Archer* included a number of names that since have become legend in field and hunting archery circles. Big are the names of Roy Case, George Brommers, J. E. Davis, Kore Duryee, William "Chief" Compton, Erle Stanley Gardner, Howard Hill, Forrest Nagler, Saxton Pope, Paul Klopsteg, Cassius Styles, Ken and Walt Wilhelm, Earl L. Ullrich, B. G. Thompson, Art Young, and John Yount.

A major landmark in bowhunting history was established in September, 1930, when archers from widely scattered areas converged on the Lower Rogue River, Curry County, Oregon. If hope and enthusiasm could be measured in terms of venison, they would have returned home loaded with meat. However, according to Earl Ullrich, one of the participants, they had to settle for one lone "wild pig" that fell victim to the broadhead of one of the Robin Hoods. When not prowling the timber for game, they challenged one another to compete on the roving course improvised for their pleasure by Ullrich who fashioned targets from cartons and gunny sacks. It is doubtful that these pioneer hunters really suspected the magnitude of the bowhunting movement they were helping unveil.

This was the first known archery hunters' jamboree with a national flavor.

It was at this "jamboree" that discussions regarding organizing an association of hunting archers first were held. Two years later, these dreams came true with the informal organizing of the American Broad-Arrow Society. That year Maude Rolf Stover, then temporary editor of *Ye Sylvan Archer,* wrote:

The American Broad-Arrow Society is developing satisfactorily. The Society as planned is to be in the nature of an honorary association, open to field and hunting archers who are true sportsmen, devoted to the bow as a hunting weapon and with proper regard for wildlife and game conservation.

Special chipped arrowheads were awarded successful member bowhunters. There were no dues, and membership was secured by merely "signing up." Such was the state of affairs during the depth of the great depression of the early 1930's, when time meant little and money was most difficult to come by.

B. G. Thompson, chairman of the group that organized the American Broad-Arrow Society in 1932, in *Ye Sylvan Archer* wrote in part that:

> The organization of the Broad-Arrows [sic] Society has been rather slow, due to the fact that interested parties have been so far removed from each other. However, the committee has adopted a constitution and has the organization pretty well rounded into shape.

An editorial in the same issue stated that the charter members of the organization then numbered in the hundreds.

This group of bowhunting pioneers included many prominent business and professional men whose words carried a lot of weight everywhere, including legislative halls. Their pioneering effort probably was the major factor that led to the legalizing of hunting with bow and arrow in various states, and then to securing preseasons for bowhunting in Wisconsin (1934) and Michigan (1937), and a special bowhunting refuge area in Oregon (1934).

The Broad-Arrow Society was handicapped by not having anyone who could afford to devote the amount of time and effort necessary for successful promotion. Accordingly, the society "faded," as it failed to gain national recognition on a lasting basis.

Another important event in the movement for field archery was the formation of the Art Young Foundation in 1936. It was organized by a host of archery friends of the late Arthur Young, famous bowhunter, who had died unexpectedly in 1935. The guiding hand of Dr. Paul Klopsteg, a nationally recognized author of archery articles, was most important in this event, which proved to be the forerunner to a movement to organize Art Young field clubs on a national basis. The movement, however, stalled.

That Young was highly regarded by fellow archers is obvious by events following his death. What many may not know is that he was regarded with reverence by such prominent pioneer archers as "Chief" Compton, an archery giant in his own right.

Saxton Pope, a frequent hunting companion of Young, was equally famous and highly regarded. Pope's book *Hunting with the Bow and Arrow,* which first appeared in 1923, had a widespread influence on the sporting public.

Stories about the exploits of these pioneer field archers in Africa, Alaska, and America added lure to the sport of bowhunting (Fig. 13–1). Is it any wonder that their names were combined to designate the Pope-Young Round in archery.

The year 1936 witnessed the formation of the statewide Pope-Young Field Archers of Oregon at Portland, honoring both these famous bowhunters. A constitution prepared by Earl Ullrich was adopted with the

Fig. 13–1. The late Art Young, famous pioneering field and hunting archer, is here shown with a lion he shot on his historic African hunt with Dr. Saxton Pope. He proved once again that a bow is an effective hunting weapon. (By permission from *Archery*, by R. P. Elmer. Copyright, 1926, Tudor Publishing Co.; New York.)

first tournament scheduled for Labor Day, September 7, 1936, at Roseburg.

While the Pope-Young Round promoted by this organization found ready acceptance in that state and is still enjoyed as an annual shoot in Oregon, it did not represent a clean break from the more traditional target-type archery. The round still utilized open spaces and conventional-type targets.

Activities of the freedom-loving Oregon archers took them more and more afield. Their love for roving and less-formalized bowshooting helped popularize bowhunting, which got special concession in Oregon in 1934. Theirs was the first special bow and arrow deer hunting preserve established in the United States.

The biggest single landmark along the way to the formation of a national field organization was the formation of the Southern California Field Archers on January 24, 1937. Field shooters of southern California had been invited to Redlands for a roving shoot jointly sponsored by the Redlanders and the Los Angeles Art Young Archers.

John Yount who became the first secretary of the new organization initiated a column in *Ye Sylvan Archer*. He reported that fifty-eight archers competed at a subsequent shoot at the Redlands "Rover" Course, with Howard Hill, later to become a famous motion picture archer, winning the gold medal. Yount's column, which covered news and views, appeared regularly until the formation of the N.F.A.A. 2 years later. His enthusiastic reports of happenings in the Southern California Field Archers Association did much to pave the way for the formation of a national organization that was soon to follow.

By mid-summer of 1937, it was obvious that field archery was rapidly gaining strength. The only question remaining to be determined was, what national organization would control it? The National Archery Association at first was reluctant to let the field archers go their own way. Rebelling field shooters, however, were equally determined to organize and run their own and separate organization.

The year 1939 became the biggest of all in the history of field archery. Klopsteg, president of the National Archery Association, appointed a field committee of six men to study the question of cooperation between field and target archers. August of that year saw the official beginning of the N.F.A.A. with publication of a temporary constitution. This was the very year that field archers had been granted their wish to organize their own and separate field events at the NAA Tournament at St. Paul, Minnesota.

The first charter member of the N.F.A.A. was George Brommers, who on August 4, 1939, paid fifty cents in dues to John Yount. After all the prodding, needling, and writing to support such a move, it was most fitting for Brommers to secure this distinction.

Thirty days after initiating a membership drive, there existed nineteen field courses in California, three in Texas, three in Michigan, one in Ohio, and one in Virginia.

Following the 1939 National Target Tournament, Henry Cummings as president of the NAA appointed a field committee that eased the transition of field archery from the NAA to the emerging N.F.A.A. Field archers now had their own organization.

The first elected officers and regional representatives of the formally organized N.F.A.A. were installed in the fall of 1940. They included A. J. Michelson as president, Paris B. Stockdale as vice-president, and John Yount as secretary-treasurer. Regional representatives included H. C. Macquarrie of California, Fred Bear of Michigan, and T. C. Davison of New Jersey.

By February, 1941, twenty-four states had affiliated with the N.F.A.A. Archers of the West, especially Oregon, had contributed much to the success of the organization (Fig. 13–2).

So ended the long and uphill struggle of field and hunting archers to organize their own national organization, the N.F.A.A., an organization independent of the older and well-established NAA. Things were really shaping up, but there was a war on that had to be successfully concluded before archers could fully enjoy their new-found sport.

Fig. 13–2. It was a historic group of bowhunters that gathered in 1941 at Dr. B. G. Thompson's cabin near Corvallis, Oregon They were (1) Chester Stevenson, (2) Claude Lampert, (3) Sid Claypool, (4) Ken Shoemaker, (5) Norman Theberath, (6) Bill Williams, (7) Med Meyers, (8) Howard Knight, (9) Howard Dixon, (10) George Golden, (11) Henry Hewitt, and (12) John Davis. (Photograph courtesy of C. Stevenson.)

When looking back, it appears that organizational activities were largely the efforts of John Yount, John Davis, B. G. Thompson, F. Nagler, P. Stockdale, J. Cooter, and G. Brommers. The first three were most prominent in the limelight. Brommers, however, is not to be passed up lightly. He had a faculty for working behind scenes, needling a little here, encouraging a little there, and thus influencing others to greater efforts. He was a master at such strategy up to the very time of his death in 1956. It is little wonder that he was awarded the N.F.A.A.'s first Compton Medal of Honor in 1947. He was an important link between the archery of Pope, Young, and Compton and the beginning of field archery and bowhunting as we know them today. His guiding hand was heavy, steady, and sometimes a little rough.

Without the foresight and able leadership of these promoters, the formation of the N.F.A.A. would certainly have been delayed until after World War II. The developing of the sport of bowhunting would thus certainly have been delayed at least a decade.

The difference between the success of the N.F.A.A. and the blossoming and fading of the American Broad-Arrow Society probably resulted from the difference in enthusiasm and organizational ability of one couple. That couple was John and Vera Yount. John continued to carry the burden as secretary-treasurer of the N.F.A.A. until November, 1958, when he resigned. Even as early as 1943, his efforts were appreciated by such famous men as Erle Stanley Gardner, an ardent field and hunting archer. Gardner's message to Yount was as follows:

Lots of the best, and congratulations to you for your untiring devotion and loyalty to archery. It's some of you fellows who keep plugging along that makes it possible for a lot of the rest of us to derive a lot of enjoyment. More power to you.

GROWTH OF THE N.F.A.A.

A year after its beginning in 1939, the N.F.A.A. had a membership of 300. By 1942 there were 906; and by 1943, members numbered 1,350. This healthy growth over the first 4-year period—a period plagued by World War II—is quite surprising. It was certainly an indication of the natural attraction of the sport. The rapid climb in membership continued through 1947 (Fig. 13–3).

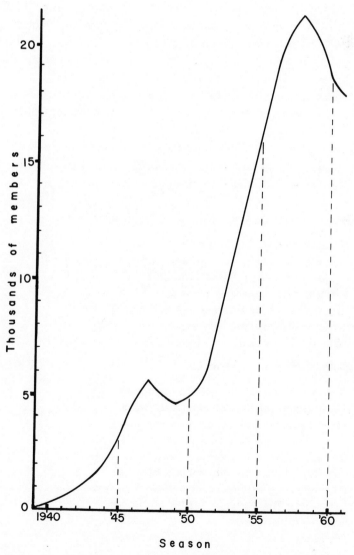

Fig. 13–3. Membership in the National Field Archery Association.

A temporary break in growth occurred in 1948. This setback is believed to have resulted from two causes. The first was a rebellion on the part of "bare-bow" (instinctive) archers with the subsequent formation of the short-lived "Instinctors, Inc." The second possible cause was the onset of the Korean conflict. In any event, the setback was short in duration as it only lasted through 1951. That was also about the end of the period of existence of the California-conceived "Instinctors, Inc." association.

Starting in 1952, and extending through 1957, there occurred a very rapid rise in membership. Increase in membership of the association, however, finally reached a peak of 21,370 in 1958. A slight decrease occurred in 1959, 1960, and 1961. The membership in 1961 was 16 per cent below the peak reached 3 years earlier.

It was under the leadership of President James Kinnee of Wisconsin that the N.F.A.A. experienced its most vigorous growth. Kinnee's term of office (1953–1956) was one of conservatism, with emphasis on bowhunting and with strict adherence to provisions of the original constitution of the N.F.A.A.

The setback in membership began with the administration of Karl Palmatier. Numerous changes in regulations and increased emphasis on sight shooting (free-style) competition marked this period.

State archery deer hunting license sales also slowed up during this period, suggesting some type of "archery recession." There is also the possibility that some archers were switching their membership to one of the newer bowhunting organizations.

Presidents of the N.F.A.A. since its organization include:

A. J. Michelson, Flint, Michigan, 1939–1948
A. O. Haugen, Lansing, Michigan and Auburn, Alabama, 1949–1950
William Morrissey, Flint, Michigan, 1951–1952
James Kinnee, Milwaukee, Wisconsin, 1953–1956
Karl Palmatier, Hickory Corners, Michigan, 1957–1960
Richard Freeman, Midland, Michigan, 1961–1962
Gilbert Boening, San Antonio, Texas, 1963–

A chronology of major developments and events in the N.F.A.A. follows:

1939   George Brommers becomes first member.
       Temporary constitution adopted.
1940   First regular constitution adopted.
       First permanent officers elected.
       Ye Sylvan Archer became first official magazine with John Davis as
         editor. Magazine and membership—$1.00.
       First official tournament in field archery (mail).
       Art Young Big Game Award established.
1941   Stump emblem adopted.
       Presidents column in official magazine started.

1942 First handbook issued by association.

20-pin award adopted.

1943 Flint Round established.

A. T. Wallis, Washington, became editor of *Ye Sylvan Archer*.

1944 *Archery* became official magazine with Roy Hoff as editor.

Small Game Award established.

1945 Gold and Silver Arrow awards adopted as supplementary awards in hunting.

Order of the Bone established.

1946 First National Field Archery Tournament at Allegan, Michigan. 476 contestants. Largest modern archery tournament to date.

1947 Perpetual Trophies of Silver for men's and women's divisions acquired.

Compton Medal of Honor established. First award to George Brommers.

Good Sportsmanship Award established. First awarded to Nubbie Pate.

1949 Arrow weights in the Hunters Field and Broadhead Rounds in force since 1946 eliminated.

1950 Sight (Free-style) Division added.

Prize Buck Award established.

1951 Instinctor rebellion. "Instinctors, Inc." organized by rebelling bare-bow archers.

1953 Landowners Guarantee to improve hunter conduct and to improve farmer-landowner-sportsman relations.

1956 Heavy Tackle Division added to National Tournament.

1960 Modified Flint Round adopted.

A FIELD ARCHERY ROUND EMERGES

Roving archery games probably were enjoyed in ages long past. Organized rules for such games of roving, however, seem to have been lost in time, if indeed such games ever existed on a scale any greater than the local tribal or band basis.

There is no way of knowing how far back into antiquity the sport of roving with bow and arrow dates. Obviously it dates back almost to the beginning of the bow and arrow itself. Before stone-age man tackled animals with his bow, he probably had done considerable shooting at various marks such as tufts of grass, rotten logs or stumps, buffalo "chips," or similar marks to gain accuracy and confidence in his shooting ability. This truly was field archery in the beginning. Accordingly, in the beginning, all archery was bare-bow, "field-type" archery.

Ishi, the last Yahi (Yana) Indian, made famous through the writings of Saxton Pope, did his best shooting at small objects, the size of quail. His archery, like the archery of primitive peoples before him, was instinctive archery in the truest sense.

New archery games were already appearing in the mid-twenties. C. S.

Knight, writing in *Ye Sylvan Archer* in 1927, described three games played with bow and arrow. They included "Arrow Golf" (later called archery golf), "Arrowkay" (a croquette-like game with bow and arrow), and "Pegs and Points." Archery golf had already found favor in the hearts of many archers as a result of having been shot quite extensively in Ohio and at the Michigan State Medical Society meetings at Mackinac Island, Michigan, in June, 1927.

One of the major sources of influence on the game of field archery as we know it today may well have been the roving range established at the Summer Resort of George Robinson near Frankfort, Michigan. Robinson is a real old-timer in archery, having started shooting a bow in 1877. In 1929 he started laying out a roving course, which was completed in 1931. This certainly was the earliest permanent field layout in the Midwest, and possibly in the nation. It consisted of a series of thirty-nine targets in the forest-covered sand hills at his resort. Distances of his targets, which ranged from 25 feet to 70 yards, are remarkably similar to the distances of the modern field round. Feed sacks stuffed with excelsior and with 4-inch bull's-eyes served as targets. Robinson's layout was his own idea and was independent of the Michigan Archers Association. That organization, however, did hold a 2-day tournament there in 1938, at which meet twenty-five archers competed.

The existence and popular acceptance of that course was recorded in the March, 1933, *Archery Review* by Professor Oren F. Evans of Norman, Oklahoma. Evans' article reads as follows:

There is no pleasanter sport for an archer than shooting over a good roving course and if archery is ever to reach the degree of popularity of some other sports it will probably be through roving rather than pure target practice. It was my good fortune last summer to have the opportunity to shoot over what I consider an ideal roving course, and I would like to pass on to my fellow archers a chance to share my good fortune.

I met Mr. Robinson at the Michigan State Tournament last summer, and a few days later I visited him at his place on the south side of Crystal Like near Frankfort, Michigan. He has a large beautifully wooded property facing the lake through which he has laid out a roving course with 39 targets. The course winds about through the hills and valleys so that each target is a surprise as to elevation and distance. Also they are placed so that there is a bank behind each target. In going over the course three of us shot about 200 arrows, each without injury or loss of arrows. The woods are delightfully cool and there are two or three springs with cool, pure water along the course.

Mr. Robinson is always glad to welcome archers and himself enjoys shooting over the course with them. The course is not being run for profit. No charge at all was being made last summer but I think a charge of $0.25 per day is to be made the coming summer which is hoped will be about enough to pay for keeping the targets . . .

If we had more courses of this kind it would be a great help to archery.

Author Haugen had the pleasure of examining this roving course in 1946, at which time some of the targets and paths were still in evidence. Maintenance had been discontinued in 1939, the very year in which the N.F.A.A. was organized. The targets were suspended on wires between stakes or trees. It was indeed in a beautiful setting. The few targets shot at the time were as challenging as any of the targets on present-day field courses.

Robinson confided that his wife had thought he wasted too much time working on the archery layout. Accordingly he used to get up real early in the morning, well before anyone else would arise, and worked on the course when no one could tell how much time he spent there. A few other archers have done similarly for their sport, but they add up to only about 5 per cent of those participating in the sport. Robinson was still an archery promoter at the ripe old age of 96, at which age he had practiced the sport for 80 years (Fig. 13–4).

Fig. 13–4. The late George Robinson of Traverse City, Michigan, who started shooting a bow in 1877, here at the age of 92 is coaching one of the many people he introduced to archery. (Photograph courtesy of G. Robinson.)

Indications are that the field archery round as we know it today evolved mainly from experiments at the Redlands Archery Club at Redlands, California, starting in 1934. Though target archers by earlier experience, the Redlanders yearned for more variety and less formality in archery. Instead of just lamenting about their lack of interest in target rounds, and quitting, they solved their own problem by inventing a new round to satisfy their desires. They combined the best ideas on roving-type archery to date, added a lot of original ideas, and after much cutting and trying came out with a proposed field round. Much of this cutting and trying was done in an arroyo at the John Yount place at Redlands. After building and rebuilding a series of seven courses, the club in 1936 had established a field round that was quite similar to the one still in use by field archers everywhere. The Redlanders and the Art Young Archers of Los Angeles jointly had contributed much toward the new-type round developed. Their many invitational tournaments on courses at Redlands and at El Segundo, California, did much to iron out weaknesses in the initial experimental layouts. Their activities also had much to do with welding together ideas and the people who provided the vanguard to the formation of a national organization.

A few other states had also been interested in some types of field shooting in the 1930's but without the benefit of standardized rounds except for archery golf, which gained a good following in Ohio. That game is discussed in Chapter 3.

Oregon's first tournament, which in any way approached a statewide field shoot, was held September 2–4, 1933, using targets representing animals ranging in size from squirrels to lions. Distances of the shots ranged from 10 to 180 yards. First prize, which consisted of a silver medal, went to the man with the most hits—George Brommers. This is the only reference found regarding Brommers' shooting. He usually devoted his whole time to promoting archery and encouraging others.

14

Development of
Modern Bowhunting

The sport of bowhunting is a conservation measure for three important reasons. First, it permits a maximum of recreation at little or no expense to the deer herd. In fact, the combined kill by bow and arrow in Michigan, Wisconsin, Pennsylvania, Minnesota, and Iowa in 1960 was slightly less than one-third the kill by vehicles that same year in those states (Table 14–1). Second, it makes it possible to harvest game in thickly settled areas where use of gunfire may be unsafe or not tolerated by residents. An arrow that narrowly misses its mark in deer and rabbit hunting will nearly always bury itself harmlessly in the ground within a few yards beyond the animal. Third, bowhunting permits recreational use of game populations that may not be large enough to permit extensive harvest such as occurs in gun seasons.

TABLE 14–1

Comparison of Kill of Deer by Vehicles and by Bow and Arrow in a Sample of States in 1960

State	Kill by Vehicles	Kill by Archers
Michigan	3,150	1,600
Wisconsin	3,038	1,091
Pennsylvania	7,187	1,163
Minnesota	1,354	445
Iowa	546	277
Total	15,275	4,576

Both stalk-hunting and still-hunting along deer runways require that deer be as undisturbed as possible. Such conditions are most apt to occur where the bow season precedes the gun season. Separate seasons for bow and gun hunting for deer are also desirable from the standpoint of safety to the oft-camouflaged and/or stalking bowhunter. Such a method of hunting is not considered safe during gun seasons. Bagging your deer by

153

stalking offers a greater thrill than can be gained from any other method of hunting. Why not join the crowd of bowhunters and find out for yourself? (Fig. 14–1.)

Fig. 14–1. Many of today's hundreds of thousands of bowhunters began as big-game gun hunters. (Courtesy of O. Warbach.)

MODERN BOWHUNTING UNFOLDS: THE BIG SEVEN

Bow and arrow big-game hunting got its first major boost in the mid-thirties when Wisconsin, Oregon, and Michigan made new and separate provisions for deer hunting in their respective states (Fig. 14–2). A short review of the chronology of bow and arrow hunting in what may be regarded as the "Big Seven" states seems appropriate. These states include Wisconsin, Oregon, Michigan, Pennsylvania, New York, California, and Minnesota. The choice of these states for more detailed consideration was made on the basis of numbers of bowhunters.

Bowhunting in Wisconsin started in 1930 when Roy Case of Racine received a special permit from conservation authorities to hunt with bow and arrow in the regular gun season. On December 6 of that season, Case bagged his buck, the first bow and arrow–killed deer in Wisconsin in modern times (Fig. 14–3).

The first separate preseason for deer in Wisconsin, in fact in any state, was provided in 1934. The hunt was set for 5 days in two counties. Conservation authorities subsequently reported that the participants were a small group, viewed tolerantly, regarded as queer, and at times were ridiculed. One buck was bagged that first special preseason. Wisconsin's bowhunters increased from 40 registrants in 1934 to an estimated 15,000 in

Fig. 14–2. Oh relax, they're just giving the country back to the Indians.
(Courtesy of O. Warbach.)

Fig. 14–3. Veteran bowhunter Roy Case of Racine, Wisconsin, with the buck
he killed on December 6, 1930, in Vilas County, a first for Wisconsin. (Photograph courtesy of R. Case.)

1950. A total of about 25,000 participated in the 1956 season. The two biggest boosts to bowhunting in Wisconsin occurred with the adding of antlerless deer to the legal game list in 1943, and the opening of the Necedah National Wildlife Refuge to bowhunting for deer in 1945.

Oregon was one of the "early-bird" states in bowhunting. The bow had been a legal weapon until 1921 when a revision of laws outlawed all weapons except rifles, shotguns, and pistols. Bows, however, again became legal weapons in the gun season in 1927. Three years later, in 1930, a group of twenty-three archers from Oregon, California, Washington, and Wisconsin congregated in Oregon to participate in the first organized New World bowhunt with a national flavor. In 1934, the Canyon Creek Archery Area was established, the first bowhunting preserve set aside in the nation. This provision for bowhunting permitted the taking of a deer of either

Fig. 14–4. One of the three bucks taken at Blaney Park, Michigan, in 1931 was bagged by the late Herman Stroud of Wayland, Michigan. It weighed 200 lbs. dressed. (Photograph courtesy of H. Stroud.)

sex, a most liberal provision for that period. By 1954, bowhunters in Oregon had increased to 4,464.

Michigan got its major start in bowhunting in 1937 when a special preseason was established. That year, 186 archers participated. Popularity of the sport literally mushroomed as regulations were liberalized in the years that followed. The number of bowhunters reached a peak at 42,356 in 1956. One of the earliest Michigan bowhunters was Herman Stroud of Wayland (Fig. 14–4). Other successful bowhunters were H. J. Cooper of Kalamazoo and Ted Abrahms of Lansing.

The biggest boost to bowhunting in Michigan came in 1941 when the first special season was opened in Allegan County. That season made it possible to take a deer of either sex for the first time. This liberalization did much to encourage bowhunting (Figs. 14–5 to 14–8).

Fig. 14–5. Dorr Sweet of Muskegon, Michigan, is the proud archer who bagged this 312-lb. (live weight) buck, the first taken in Michigan's Allegan State Forest when the season was opened there in 1941. (Photograph by Carl Gower.)

Fig. 14–6. Jack Yaeger, one of the real old-timer's in Michigan bowhunting, took this 263-lb. (dressed weight) buck in the Allegan State Forest in 1942.

Fig. 14–7. Preparing for a hunt in 1943 at Allegan, Michigan, are H. Eldridge and Charles Laird of Mendon. Strings were checked, arrows straightened, and broadheads sharpened by filing to produce a fine-toothed edge. They tented at Allegan's famous "Nudist Camp."

Fig. 14–8. Alma and Wesley Blundell of Muskegon, Michigan, belong with Michigan's old-time successful bowhunters. They were both successful at Allegan in 1943. Look who took the bigger deer.

Pennsylvania legalized bow and arrow hunting for game in 1929, then established two separate game preserves for bowhunting in 1937 (Fig. 14–9). These preserve areas continued until 1951 when they were replaced by more liberal regulations for the sport. The new regulations provided for a special statewide season for archery deer hunting. Further liberalization occurred in 1957 when does and fawns were added to the fair-game list.

Participation in Pennsylvania bow and arrow deer hunts remained limited through the 1930's and 1940's. In the 1950's, however, participation increased by leaps and bounds, skyrocketing to 76,767 hunters in 1959.

California bowhunters had to compete with gun hunters until 1945 when a 10-day preseason was provided. Antlerless deer in the Golden Bear State first became legal in 1949. An estimated 28,500 archers enjoyed bowhunting in 1957.

New York issued 853 bowhunting licenses in 1948, the first special season for archery deer hunting. That season provided for 2 weeks of hunting for bucks only. The real effort to secure this season had been initiated 2 years earlier. Authority to take a deer of either sex was added by the 1952 legislature, with the result that the popularity of bowhunting rose considerably. Participation reached its peak of 25,809 in 1957.

Minnesota, although it permitted bowhunting as early as 1929, first

Fig. 14–9. History-making Pennsylvania bowhunters in about 1929. Left to right are Harold Stahle now of Cumberland, Merwin Crownover, and James Fentress, then of the Harrisburg area. (Photograph courtesy of *Pennsylvania Game News.*)

made special provisions for bowhunting in 1940. In that year a separate preseason was provided in Itasca County. The sale of 12,321 licenses in 1960 indicates a small but continued upward trend in participation in the sport.

The general trend in bowhunting in the nation since it got its major start in the mid-thirties indicates a rapid increase in popularity. Rise in popularity was greatest from about 1951 through 1957 (Fig. 14–10). A slowup in license sales for bow and arrow deer hunting, however, first appeared in Michigan that year. Since then several of the other more important bowhunting states have also suffered setbacks in license sales. The trend in each of the states examined for license sales was so consistently downward in 1958–1960 that it is obvious the sport of bowhunting was in a slump.

Was this drop in popularity due to an economic recession? Was it due to the swing toward boating as the popular hobby? Or, was it the result of the extremely critical antibowhunting articles that first appeared in 1959? The latter possibility is probably not the major influence because the slowup in growth, and in some cases a decrease in numbers, had already occurred before the critical articles appeared. This was especially true in Michigan, California, and New York.

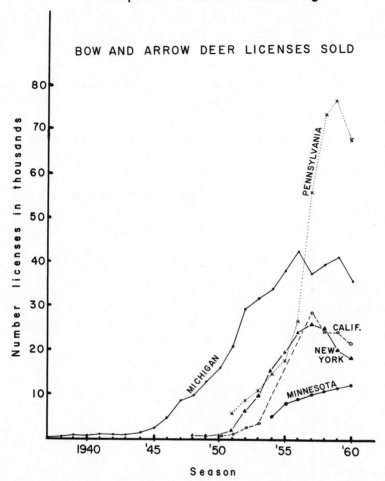

Fig. 14–10. Bowhunting license sales in some of the leading bow and arrow deer hunting states.

THE HARVEST OF DEER

The harvest of deer by bow and arrow in various states remained insignificant in numbers until the mid-forties. By insignificant is meant fewer than 100 deer in any one state in any one season.

Wisconsin was the first state to exceed this magic number in its harvest of deer with the bow. It did so in 1945 when the Necedah National Wildlife Refuge first was opened to deer hunting. A kill of 61 deer was secured in the Refuge, and an additional 99 in other parts of the state that year.

Michigan archers a year later, in 1946, also exceeded the 100-deer mark, with a take of 168. Oregon (1951), New York (1952), Utah (1954), California (1954), Minnesota (1954), and Pennsylvania (1955) next cracked the 100-deer mark.

It is Michigan and Wisconsin that have dominated the field in number of deer harvested with bow and arrow over the years. The peak in the kill of deer in both states occurred in 1958, when archers in these states bagged 2,600 and 1,885 respectively (Fig. 14–11).

The harvest of deer in New York took a rapid upturn in 1952, Utah in 1955, and in Pennsylvania in 1957. The annual take in Minnesota and California has remained much smaller, leveling off at between 250 and 400 deer. The most startling increase in kill of deer occurred in Pennsylvania with the take rising from 224 deer in 1956 to 1,358 in 1957. A similar rapid rise in harvest occurred in Utah, increasing from 290 in 1955 to 1,820 deer in 1959.

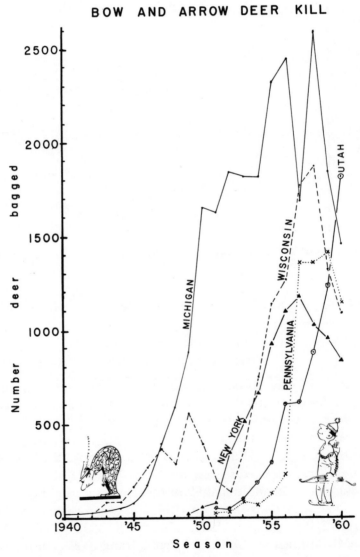

Fig. 14–11. Kill of deer in some leading bowhunting states. (Cartoon figures courtesy of O. Warbach.)

The title of "superproducers" belongs to the states yielding the highest percentages of hunter success. Colorado, for instance, in 1957 led the nation with a kill success of 20.5 per cent (roughly one out of each five hunters successful) but had to settle for 16 per cent in 1959. Utah archers with a kill of 1,820 deer in 1960 yielded a kill success of 19.9 per cent. In 1958, 12.4 per cent of Iowa's archers were successful; a year later Hawkeye State archers upped their success to 16.2 per cent.

Success in the "Big Seven" bowhunting states (those with the greatest number of bowhunters) in 1959 amounted to: New York—4.7 per cent, Michigan—4.6, Wisconsin—5.3, Minnesota—3.3, Pennsylvania—2.0, and California—1.2 per cent. Oregon's success in 1954 amounted to 6.6 per cent. Year to year fluctuations to the extent of about 1 per cent are not uncommon. Accordingly, these states with the largest numbers of bow-hunters are not among the best producers in terms of percentages of hunters successful.

This is not to imply that the real reward from bowhunting depends on the percentage of hunters who bring home venison. On the contrary, it is the sport and recreational benefits that count. As an example of the amount of recreation provided by bowhunting, Iowa's 1,627 archers in 1959 enjoyed an average of 41 hours of recreation in hunting. Another way to look at it is that 252 hours of recreation were provided for each of the 255 deer harvested. This truly is a case of providing a maximum of recreation with a limited resource. Bowhunting, accordingly, almost amounts to enjoying the pleasure of eating one's cake and having it too. It is a way for the hunter to get closer to nature (Fig. 14–12).

Fig. 14–12. The spirit of bowhunting is at its best in the wilderness, for in wilderness there is peace and solitude, with a naturalness of things. May there always be wilderness and the sportsmanship that is most apt to prevail there. Lake of the Clouds, Porcupine Mountains, Michigan.

BIG-GAME AWARDS

The Art Young Big Game Award was adopted in 1940 by the N.F.A.A. The idea of such an award first had been conceived by the Art Young Foundation, an organization established by friends of Young, a famous archer, bowhunter, and writer who had died as a relatively young man in 1935. As sponsored by the N.F.A.A., the purpose of this award is to promote interest in bowhunting, to encourage good sportsmanship, and to give recognition by organized field archers to their members who obtain game with the bow (Fig. 14–13).

Fig. 14–13. A measure of both pride and satisfaction is due any bowhunter lucky enough to bag an outstanding trophy animal such as this caribou taken by Fred Bear of Michigan. It is indeed worthy of an Art Young Big Game Award. (Photograph courtesy of F. Bear.)

During the earlier years of the N.F.A.A., big-game awards were presented for any one of the larger animals such as deer, elk, moose, antelope, caribou, goat, sheep, leopard, panther, cougar, bear, lynx, bobcat, wolf, coyote, wild boar, javelina, turkey, alligator, crocodile, and feral pigs, but not including the young of these species. In 1958, the wolf, javelina, turkey, bobcat, lynx, and coyote were transferred from the big-game to the small-game list and now qualify a lucky archer for full small-game awards. Other small-game animals bagged, including alligators and crocodiles, contribute toward a point system for earning small-game awards. The bagging of feral domestic animals no longer qualifies an archer for an award. Details on both big- and small-game awards are listed in the *N.F.A.A. Official Handbook of Field Archery.*

To qualify an archer for an award, game animals must be taken under sporting conditions. In adopting a rule for fair chase, the N.F.A.A. endeavored to encourage and foster the highest possible level of sportsmanship in the ranks of bowhunters. Any hunter who shoots an animal under any of the unfavorable conditions enumerated in the Fair Chase Rule (given below) either has no conscience or has one that is a bit too calloused for the good of the sport. Nevertheless, such calloused conduct has occurred on several occasions in recent years.

BOWHUNTER FAIR CHASE RULE

No Art Young Big Game Award will be considered for animals taken under any of the following conditions:

1. Helpless in or because of deep snow
2. Helpless in water, on ice, or in a trap
3. While confined behind fences as on game farms, etc.
4. By "Jack Lighting" or shining at night
5. In defiance of game laws or out of season
6. From a power vehicle or power boat
7. By any other means considered by the N.F.A.A. as unsportsmanlike.

Through June of 1961, a total of 12,141 Big Game Awards has been made by the N.F.A.A. It all began with a single award in 1940 and continued in modest numbers of fewer than a hundred per year through World War II. Following the Korean Conflict in the early 1950's, numbers of awards increased to a peak of 1,384 in 1958 (Fig. 14–14). The decrease in awards since that time probably results from two influences; namely, a decrease in N.F.A.A. membership and a reduction in number of species that qualify for an award.

WHO'S WHO AMONG WOMEN BOWHUNTERS

In a general way, women have remained unsung heroes in the history of big-game bowhunting. Men have been so busy promoting, hunting, and reporting on their archery prowess that they have overlooked the contributions and accomplishments of the fairer sex—the Lady Dianas. George Brommers, one of the early organizers of field archery, paid his respects to the fairer sex with the comment that without the active support of the ladies, Oregon would never have reached its prominent archery status.

Many women bowhunters face up to all the tasks of a hunt and do not

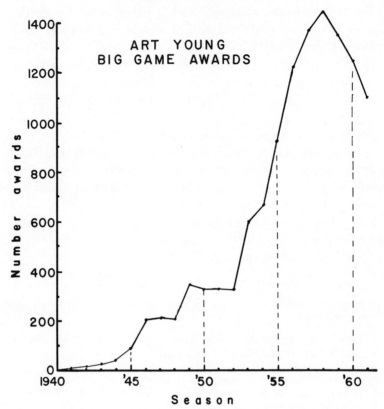

Fig. 14–14. Number of Art Young Big Game Awards presented by the N.F.A.A.

hesitate one bit when it comes to the job of cleaning their animal once it has been felled with an arrow. Personal observations over the years also have convinced the authors that most women archers insist on shooting their own deer and do not let "hubby" do it.

In an attempt to do justice where justice is due, a special honor roll of some successful women bowhunters is presented herewith. Here's to the pioneering women bowhunters of days gone by, bless them every one.

WHO'S WHO AMONG WOMEN BOWHUNTERS

Mrs. Elisabeth Rounsevelle	North Carolina	Deer	1927
Mrs. F. P. Gable	Montana	Wolverine	1931
Mrs. Edward McNish	Tennessee	Boar	1939
Mrs. Edith (Sasha) Siemel	Brazil	Cougar	1940
Mrs. Euretha Schomaker	Michigan	{ Deer	1943
		{ Cougar	1947
Mrs. Alma Blundell	Michigan	Deer	1943
Mrs. Roy Hilton	Minnesota	Deer	1943
Mrs. W. A. Burdick	Wisconsin	Deer	1943
Mrs. Grace Gisselman	Wisconsin	Deer	1943
Mrs. Sylvia Hutchinson	Minnesota	Deer	1944
Mrs. John Schoenike	Wisconsin	Deer	1944

Mrs. Peter Erickson	Wisconsin	Deer	1944
Violette Strauss	Wisconsin	Deer	1945
Anna Kjeldsen	Illinois	Deer	1945
Mrs. Edna Howatt	Washington	Deer	1946
Mrs. Bizz Lawson	Washington	Deer	1946
Mrs. Eleanor Hamilton	Ohio	Deer	1946
Mrs. Rosemary Furry	Indiana	Deer	1946
Vivian Renshaw	Michigan	Deer	1946
Mary M. Seth	Minnesota	Deer	1946
Mrs. Madeline Allen	Michigan	Deer	1947
Mrs. Verne Tritten	Utah	Cougar	1947
Mrs. Catherine Beebe	Washington	Cougar	1947
Mrs. John Coats	Wisconsin	Deer	1947
Mrs. Phil Fawver	Illinois	Deer	1947
Mrs. Ardis Hays	Michigan	Deer	1947
Mrs. Louise K. Henson	Michigan	Deer	1947
Mrs. Ezella Rearick	Michigan	Deer	1947
Laura Wilcoxson	Indiana	Deer	1947
Mrs. Farol Anderson	Indiana	Deer	1948
Mrs. Celia B. Coe	Indiana	Deer	1948
Ann Keenan	Michigan	Deer	1948
Mrs. Frances Lesonick	Michigan	Deer	1948
Evelyn Pierson	Michigan	Deer	1948
Mrs. Jane Schensted	Minnesota	Deer	1948
Mrs. Shirley Smalley	California	Deer	1948
Maxine Phillips	Washington	Deer	1948
Gladys Renk	Wisconsin	Deer	1948
Ina Diedrick	Wisconsin	Deer	1948
Mrs. Viola MacWilliams	Wisconsin	Deer	1948
Mrs. Hazel White	Michigan	Deer	1949
Mrs. Frances Lozon	Michigan	Deer	1949
Mrs. Russel Kampenga	Michigan	Deer	1949
Mrs. Lloyd Spurbeck	Michigan	Deer	1949
Mrs. Valerie Baldwin	Wisconsin	Deer	1949
Helen Raulf	Wisconsin	Deer	1949
Mrs. Daniel Brewer	Wisconsin	Deer	1949
Mrs. Ruth Imler	Arizona	Javelina	1949
Mrs. Helen Cameron	New York	Deer	1954
Mrs. Ernal Olson	Iowa	Deer	1956
Mrs. Carmen Saunders	Oregon	Elk	1958

Fig. 14—15. Euretha Schomaker of Detroit was Michigan's first successful bowhuntress. She bagged her buck at Allegan in 1943.

Fig. 14—16. Mrs. Ernal Olson, Whiting, Iowa, the first Hawkeye State woman to bag a deer with bow and arrow has just cause for that smile of satisfaction. She bagged this "button" buck in 1956. (Photograph courtesy of Mrs. Olson.)

Fig. 14–17. Mrs. Helen Cameron of Newfield, New York, was the first woman to bag a deer with bow and arrow in that state (1954). At the end of 7 years of bowhunting, she had the enviable record of having taken seven deer. (Photograph courtesy of Mrs. Cameron.)

Fig. 14–18. The first woman bowhunter to bag an elk was Mrs. Carmen Sanders of Brookings, Oregon. Her elkskin jacket came from the bull elk she took in 1958. (Photograph courtesy of Mrs. Sanders.)

Fig. 14–19. Mrs. Ed McNish was the first woman to shoot a Russian wild boar in the United States with a bow and arrow. Her boar weighed 200 lbs. It was taken in the Cherokee National Forest in the fall of 1939. (Tenn. Conservation Dept. photo.)

APPENDIXES

APPENDIX A

Teaching Aids in Field Archery

INTRODUCTION

Many schools and colleges are in need of materials on how and in what order to teach the elements of field archery. The following outline of twenty-five lessons will be useful to physical education instructors, archery counselors in camps, archery club leaders, and supervisors of archery in city recreation departments.

The lessons outlined can be easily extended or shortened to meet the needs of individual groups. These lessons have been geared to the needs of beginners in field archery. The distances used are short and the pre-draw gap system of shooting is taught. The post-draw gap system of shooting will be introduced in lessons near the end of the course.

All directions in the series of lessons are for right-handed archers. Therefore, left-handed archers must interpret instructions in reverse direction, substituting opposite arm, etc.

INFORMATION ON EQUIPMENT

It is assumed that an adequate number of suitable bows are available with drawing weights approximately 20 to 22 lbs. at 28 inches or 18 to 20 lbs. at 26 inches. It is also assumed that the following are also available:

1. Six or more straw butts at least 24 inches in diameter with uprights or target standards to support them, or six or more separate backstops each made of three bales of hay or straw wired together. Either type of backstop is suitable for supporting the target faces.

2. Twenty-four or more quivers (ground quivers or hip quivers if used outside, and floor quivers if used inside) (Fig. A–1).

3. Four or five dozen 18-inch diameter field archery target faces and four or five dozen 12-inch field archery target faces. If these faces are of paper rather than cardboard, each should be pasted, glued, or stapled to cardboard, possibly cut from the sides of large cartons.

4. About sixty wire staples to fasten the target faces to the target butts. These should be at least as stiff as wire from coat hangers from which they can be prepared. Heavier wire is even more suitable. Length of the staples should be about 6 inches.

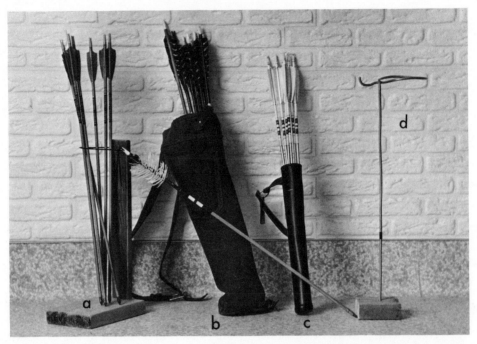

Fig. A–1. Four kinds of quivers for class use are illustrated: (*a*) floor quiver, (*b*) shoulder quiver, (*c*) belt quiver, and (*d*) ground quiver. When the wire quiver is lifted from the block, it can be pushed into the ground as far as the black tape 6 inches from the pointed bottom. Note the flu flu arrow in the foreground. This arrow is used for small game and for the "putt" in archery golf. (Photograph by Spaulding Studio, Cortland, N.Y.)

5. Preferably there should be no more than twenty-four students in one class section.

6. All bows should be marked with their bow-weights and with a serial (identification) number. When stored they should be unstrung and hung, topside up, on a numbered peg or nail corresponding to their serial number. All strings on the bows should be equipped with knots or small lumps of thread wound tightly to the serving just above the nocking point (Figs. A–2 and A–3). The bottom loop of the string may be kept in place on unstrung bows by slipping a 1-inch section of surgical rubber tubing over the string and nock area of the lower limb. Be sure it fits tightly.

7. An assortment of several dozen arrows ranging in length from 24 to 28 inches for college girls and 26 to 32 inches for college men. In a mixed class of college girls and men, it is recommended that there should be available 18 dozen arrows in the following lengths:

1 dozen arrows 24 inches	2 dozen arrows 29 inches
2 dozen arrows 25 inches	1 dozen arrows 30 inches
3 dozen arrows 26 inches	1 dozen arrows 31 inches
3 dozen arrows 27 inches	1 dozen arrows 32 inches
4 dozen arrows 28 inches	

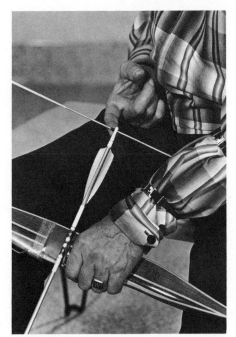

Fig. A–2. Note the single lump of thread wound and glued in place above the nocking point on the serving on the bowstring to insure consistent nocking and to prevent the arrow being accidentally brushed off the string. (Photograph by Spaulding Studio, Cortland, N.Y.)

Fig. A–3. Note the double lump or saddle-type of nocking point that holds the arrow nock somewhat more securely than does a single lump of thread. Note also the bow quiver and the nocked flu flu arrow. (Photograph by Spaulding Studio, Cortland, N.Y.)

For beginners, arrows should be approximately an inch longer than those used when the archers become experienced. This is to avoid over-drawing and shooting one's own bow hand, or drawing the arrow-pile (tip) into the belly of the bow where the arrow will splinter.

One of the best ways to determine the proper length of arrows for a particular person is to "scrape down" the belly of an old bow until it is very weak, measuring about a 10-lb. bow-weight or less at 32 inches. Drill a hole through one end of a 34- by $\frac{5}{16}$-inch dowel (birch or maple) and run a bowstring through the hole. Mark off the last foot of the other end in inches, starting from a point 24 inches from the hole in the dowel through which the string passes. The inch markers will then read 24", 25", 26", 27", 28", 29", 30", 31", 32", and 33". Then string the bow to a 6-inch "fistmele," and it is ready to use. The student should draw the string and dowel back to a full draw and anchor as indicated by the instructor who then notes the length of the dowel at the nearest full inch protruding beyond the back of the bow. The student's arrow length is therefore this nearest inch mark beyond the back of the bow (Fig. A–4).

Screw-eye through which 5/16" dowel passes

Screw-eye

34 33 32 31 30 29 28 27 | 24

├──────── 24" ────────┤

5/16"

Fig. A–4. Special light bow for determining length of arrow archer should use.

LESSON I

OBJECT: To define archery terms and to determine proper arrow length for students.

1. Explain field archery and the kinds of sports involved (field archery rounds, hunting, and roving) and the differences between field and target archery.*
2. Discuss different parts of bow and arrow and necessary archery terms (Fig. A–5).
3. Measure each student for arrows of proper length so that each can purchase a set of his own before the next class period; or if school arrows are available, assign them for use during the course. Although only four arrows are used to score in field archery, require the students to purchase or assign each at least six arrows. The two extras will save the class much time in case an arrow is broken or lost.

LESSON II

OBJECT: To learn how to unstring and string bows.

1. Have all bows to be used properly braced (strung) before the class starts.
2. Demonstrate and explain the proper method of unstringing and stringing a bow. (It is easier to learn to unstring a bow first, and then learn how to string it.)

* For information about field archery and related activities, see Part I.

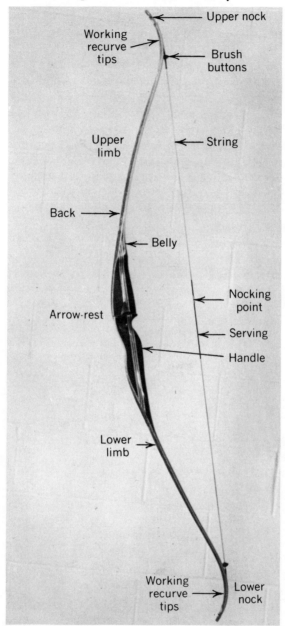

Fig. A–5. The principal parts of a bow.

3. Arrange the class (of twenty-four) in buddies or partners (A and B) in a double semicircle; the A buddies in the inner circle, with a 6-foot space between each student; instructor in the middle. Give a strung bow to all the A's so that they can go through the steps with you one at a time. The B's should serve as instructors for their buddies (to check them and see that they follow instructions). The instructor can turn his back on the group (so right- and left-handedness can be kept straight) and demonstrate steps

that the class will follow on his directions. After the second demonstration, the instructor presents the following steps, which the A's in the group carry out step by step in learning to unstring the bow.

a) Each stands with his feet parallel and a comfortable distance apart (try standing with feet apart the distance of the width of one's hips).

b) Grasp the bow at the handle with the left hand, with the back of the bow facing you, string away from you, and the arm straight out in front.

c) Swing arm and bow across the body to the right as far as it will go and lower the back of the lower nock and tip of bow into the instep of the left foot. The bow and left thumb should be touching the front of the right thigh, and the left arm should be straight.

d) Raise the right arm and hand toward the upper nock of the bow. Separate the thumb and index finger of the right hand making a V. Place the heel of the right hand just below the upper nock of the bow so that the thumb sticks out to the left of the bow tip and the index and other fingers are to the right of the tip, and the tip of the bow appears in the middle of the V like the sights in a rifle. Both arms should be straight at all times (Figs. A–6 and A–7).

Fig. A–6. Dr. Metcalf illustrates the starting position for unstringing a bow. Note that the lower tip is protected by the instep of the left foot, both arms are straight, and the bow is touching the right thigh. (Photograph by Spaulding Studio, Cortland, N.Y.)

Fig. A–7. Side view of the starting position for unstringing a bow. Note both arms are straight, with the left arm contacting the left hip. The right shoulder is brought forward between the head and the upper bow tip preparatory to bending the bow. (Photograph by Spaulding Studio, Cortland, N.Y.)

Fig. A–8. Power is applied by bringing the straight right arm and shoulder forward against the top of the upper bow limb and pressing downward on it while twisting the upper part of the trunk vigorously to the left and at the same time pulling the bow handle upward with the left arm and shoulder. Note the slack bowstring showing the power applied. (Photograph by Spaulding Studio, Cortland, N.Y.)

Fig. A–9. Note the finger action used to pull the loop to the side, up, and out of the nock while the string is slack for unstringing the bow. (Photograph by Spaulding Studio, Cortland, N.Y.)

e) At the same time, press down with the right shoulder and hand on the upper limb of the bow (just below tip and nock); throw the right shoulder forward and twist upper trunk and head to the left away from the bow, and pull away to the left on the bow handle with the left shoulder, arm, and hand. If proper position is maintained (bow against right thigh, and both arms straight), the left arm becomes a lever (crowbar type); and the left hip becomes the fulcrum. The bow will be bent and the string will become slack (Fig. A–8). Have students practice this lever action of twisting the body away from the bow and making the string go slack several times. During this process, students should be cautioned to keep their faces and buddies away from the tip in case it slips.

f) *While the bow is bent and the string is slack,* circle the right index finger around the bow tip so that it catches the base of the upper loop of the string and pulls it to the right side of bow tip and upwards out of the upper nock of the bow so that it comes toward you circling the part of the bow below the upper nock (Fig. A–9). The bow is now unstrung, with the upper loop still circling the bow as it should at a point 5 or 6 inches below the upper nock.

To string the bow, students should assume exactly the same positions they took in steps *a, b,* and *c,* etc., except that now instead of making a V with the right thumb and index finger, the tip of the right thumb *and* the left side of the right index finger at its distal joint are both underneath the upper loop on the back of the upper limb of the bow (Fig. A–10). Now, using the same muscles as those used before (in unstringing the bow), press down on upper limb with right shoulder and heel of right hand, and pull on bow handle with left shoulder and straight left arm; and twisting body to left (lever action), and putting right shoulder forward to get better leverage, *slide upper loop upwards into the nock with right thumb and outer joint of index finger.* Before making any other moves, feel carefully with thumb and index finger to make certain that the upper loop lies completely in the nock of the bow while at the same time keeping the bow tip at arm's length away from the head. To be very sure about this important point (from a personal safety standpoint), turn the bow over so that the string is up and the back of the bow is down (Fig. A–11). In this position, one can safely raise the bow tip for a closer look to be sure that the loop is in the correct position in the upper nock.

Fig. A–10. Closeup of finger action in stringing a bow. Pressure is applied in the same way as when unstringing a bow, with the heel of the right hand and shoulder applying force to the tip. Note the end of the thumb and the second digit of the index finger behind the upper loop, sliding it upwards and into the upper nock of the bow. (Photograph by Spaulding Studio, Cortland, N.Y.)

Fig. A–11. Turn the bowstring side up and check the tip to make certain that the loop of the string is completely in the upper nock. The turning over is a safety precaution to prevent injury to the face in case the string is not properly seated in the nock and thereby accidentally lets the bow spring back to the normal unstrung position. (Photograph by Spaulding Studio, Cortland, N.Y.)

Fig. A–12. Step-through method of unstringing a bow. Note the slack bowstring caused by bending the trunk forward, levering the bow against the back of the thigh and hip. The loop can now be slipped down over the bow below the nock with the other hand. (Photograph by Spaulding Studio, Cortland, N.Y.)

Fig. A–13. Step-through method of stringing the bow. As the bow is levered forward over the rear of the thigh, the left hand slides the loop up into place in the upper nock of the bow. (Photograph by Spaulding Studio, Cortland, N.Y.)

All the time the instructor is giving these instructions to the A's, their buddies, the B's, are checking their partners carefully at each step to see that they are following the instructions.

Next the whole process should be repeated with the B's taking the strung bows and following the instructor's directions one step at a time while the A's carefully check them as they learn how properly to unstring and string the bows.

Following this the instructor should give all students in the class bows and observe them unstringing and stringing the bows, personally assisting those having any difficulties. Frequently a short person has trouble with a long bow. Bows can be exchanged with other students and adjustments thus made for height and strength.

For stringing bows with recurved tips, the step-through method is frequently used (Fig. A–12). With string forward and the bow to the back, place the right leg through from the left of bow between bow and string and hook lower bow tip over front of left leg at the ankle, and lever the belly side of the bow handle over the right thigh by pressure of right hand on back of upper tip of bow (Fig. A–13). This method if carelessly used may result in twisting the tips of recurved bow limbs out of alignment and damage the bow. Commercial "bowstringers" gadgets are now on the market; and if a school or college uses many bows with working recurve tips, it will pay to purchase one. However, without bowstringers, the first method here described is probably the best for any kind of bow; and all archers should be able to use and teach it effectively.

4. If there is still time remaining in the second lesson, review and briefly explain the seven fundamental steps in shooting the bow and arrow bare-bow style (instinctive).

LESSON III

OBJECT: To review the seven basic steps and to teach the pre-draw gap system of shooting bare-bow style.

1. Demonstrate more carefully or review the seven fundamental steps in bare-bow shooting.
    a) *Stance* (see page 11, Fig. 2–1).
    b) *Nocking the arrow* (see page 13, Fig. 2–2).
    c) *Draw* (including position of left shoulder, elbow, wrist, hand, canted bow, right elbow, wrist, hand, and three fingers of right hand on string).
    d) *Anchor* (a high anchor; anchor by "saddling" the V formed by separating the right thumb and index finger over the angle of the right jawbone; thumb underneath it; top of index finger snugly under right cheekbone and tip of this finger touching right corner of the mouth). (Figs. 2–4, 2–5, 2–6 and 2–7.)
    e) *Aiming* (both eyes open and concentrating on aiming center in the middle of the bull's-eye).
    f) *Release* (live and smooth).
    g) *Afterhold or follow-through* (Fig. 2–13).
2. Mimetic drills without bows and arrows.
    a) Arrange the class in a straight line parallel to the target line and facing the targets.
    b) Have the students face right so that their left sides are toward the targets (if right-handed).
    c) Raise both arms straight sidewards.
    d) Turn heads left so that faces look at targets over top of left fists.
    e) Bend right elbows and place right hands against faces in proper field anchor position.
        (1) This can be done by one-half the class at a time. Remaining archers serve as buddies to check anchor positions of partners.
        (2) The instructor now should go down the line, carefully checking and adjusting each student's anchor.
        (3) Give the command, "Rest," so that students can lower their arms and relax. Call for a return to the anchor position several times, however, to help them quickly get the "feel" of the correct anchor position.

3. Take bows without arrows and have class practice proper position of holding bows out toward target (left elbow in proper position rotated down and out and very slightly bent if this is necessary for the string to clear the left inner surface of arm at elbow joint). (Right elbow, of course, if person shoots left-handed.)

   Practice drawing string back (without arrow) to proper instinctive anchor for brief hold while buddy and/or instructor checks anchor and position of left arm. When drawing the bow back, have upper limb canted or tilted to the right, if right-handed, about 20 degrees. Caution everyone not to stand in front of a drawn bow.

4. Have students nock an arrow on the string properly and, with bow canted, draw string and arrow back to the field or instinctive anchor for a brief hold while being checked first by the buddy and then by the instructor. Have students let the string down carefully without releasing the arrow. Draw the string back to the correct anchor a second, third, and a fourth time. This exercise must be done only while on the shooting line.

5. Have the students stand about 7 steps from the targets and each shoot an arrow, carefully following the instructor's directions regarding the pre-draw gap system of aiming. This system is a quick and effective method of educating the bow arm and eyes for eventual automatic correct bare-bow style shooting. It is particularly advantageous for all short distances up to about 35 yards.

   a) The students should take the proper stance, *except* that the right shoulder is brought forward so that the torso (upper body) is turned to the left facing the target. They should hold the canted bow and left arm in proper position out toward the target. Because the right shoulder is forward, they will be able to take the proper three-finger grip on the string without starting to draw. The students should keep arrows, fingers, wrist, and forearm in one straight line.

   b) With both eyes open, the students should raise or lower the bow so that the top of the point of the arrow (pile) appears to be about one 12-inch diameter target face below the target. This appears to leave a vertical gap with the arrow tip determining the width of the gap. Remember that this sighting is across the tip of the arrow and not down its length, and is taken *before* the draw. That is why we call the vertical distance one target face diameter (12 inches) directly below the target the pre-draw gap (page 24, Figs. 2–11 and 2–12).

   c) Keeping the bow arm (left) steadily in this position, shift the eyes up to the middle of the aiming spot (still holding bow arm and bow in the position of original aim). Now draw the string and arrow back to proper practiced anchor with bow canted about 20 degrees. Keep steadily looking at the target spot and execute a smooth, live release by gradually increasing the contraction of the muscles that pull the shoulder blade and upper arm straight back. Have buddies assist instructor in checking shooters to see that they *do not raise or lower* the bow arm and bow while drawing back to anchor, but keep bow in the original sighting elevation. Have students shoot three more arrows, using the same techniques.

d) Retrieve the arrows, drawing them properly from the target. This is done as follows: Place the backs of the fingers of one hand (left) against the target with index finger separated from the long finger by the arrow to be drawn. With the other hand (right) palm up, grasp the arrow between the thumb and index finger and pull straight back in line with the arrow and draw it from the target. To prevent bending the arrows, grasp them with the thumb and index finger closest to the target face; never with the little finger closest to the face. The backs of the fingers of the left hand protect the target face from being unnecessarily torn in this process. Only one person should draw arrows out at a time, and all others should stand back and to the side at a safe distance. If more than one person attempts to draw them, or the watchers stand too close, they unnecessarily endanger themselves to serious facial injury from the nocks of the arrows as they are drawn out.

6. If class time permits, repeat item 5, above, shooting and retrieving four more arrows using the same system, and again from a distance of 7 steps but adjusting the pre-draw gap to fit individual needs. (If arrow goes high, lower or increase the pre-draw gap; if low, raise or decrease it.)

LESSON IV

OBJECT: To establish the pre-draw gap at 10 yards.

1. Warmup period. Warm up the shooting muscles with rubber inner-tube exercisers (three cross-cut sections of auto-tire inner tubing cut into large rubber bands at least 1 inch wide and looped together square-knot style (Fig. A–14). Adjust the bands by placing the loop at one end over or behind the right elbow, and place the loop on the other end over the base of the left thumb as though it were the handle of a bow. Stretch the rubber exerciser by drawing the right elbow back (using muscles between the shoulder blades and behind the right shoulder) and bringing the right hand back into the anchor position while slightly pushing the left shoulder sideward outward but keeping the left fist or base of thumb sighted steadily on some distant object. Relax muscles and the exerciser and repeat the draw twenty to twenty-five times.

2. Review carefully the pre-draw gap system of bare-bow shooting following the instructions given in the previous class period for the 7-step distance. Then shoot four arrows using the pre-draw gap of 6 inches or one-half of a 12-inch diameter target face below the target. If arrows go low, raise the bow by decreasing the pre-draw gap to one-third of the diameter of the 12-inch target face, or even to one-fourth a diameter below the target. If arrows go high, increase the pre-draw gap to one or perhaps one and one-half target diameters below the target. Retrieve the arrows and shoot one or more ends of four arrows each, adjusting the pre-draw gap until each student has established an elevation (providing his form is good) that will put his arrows in the bull's-eye or at least at the level of the bull's-eye.

3. With the pre-draw gap established for the distance of 7 paces, step back to 10 yards from the target, shoot an end of four arrows, using the same pre-

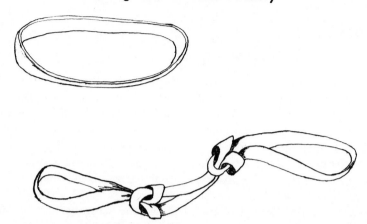

Fig. A–14. Exerciser used to develop shoulder muscles in archery. It is made from three bands of rubber cut from an auto tire inner tube and linked together square-knot style. The strength of the exerciser can be regulated by varying the width of bands used.

draw gap that worked for 7 paces, and see where the arrows go. If they go high, increase the width of the gap; and if they go low, raise and decrease the gap. Keep shooting ends of four arrows and adjusting the pre-draw gap until the proper gap is established for the new shooting distance of 10 yards. During all the shooting, the instructor should continue coaching the students and stressing proper form on each of the seven fundamentals. Check for faults to prevent establishing bad habits.

LESSON V

OBJECT: To establish pre-draw gap at 14 yards.

1. Warm up with exercisers, drawing twenty-five to thirty times.
2. Shoot one or two four-arrow ends at a 10-yard distance, checking up on form and using the pre-draw gap established for this distance during the previous class period.
3. Move back to 14 yards from the target and establish the pre-draw gap for that distance. In doing this, start with the pre-draw gap previously used at 10 yards, and do not be surprised if the same pre-draw gap used at 10 yards can also be used at the 14-yard distance. Having finally established the elevation for the pre-draw gap at 14 yards, continue shooting first at one distance (14 yards) and then the other (10 yards), and keep informal score with competition between target teams. Continue to stress good fundamental form. Stop shooting at intervals and ask students who are using good form to demonstrate before the entire class. It is in these early lessons that either bad or good habits are formed. Do not let anyone form bad habits. Have some of the better students stay with and coach individuals experiencing problems. If there are students with particularly severe problems, the instructor must work with them individually.

LESSON VI

OBJECT: To establish pre-draw gap at 17 yards.

1. Warm up by drawing the exercisers—thirty to thirty-five times.
2. Start shooting from 17 yards, using the same pre-draw gap previously used at 14 yards. It will probably be the same for both distances. Try the same pre-draw gap, giving it an honest chance for at least one end before switching to a different pre-draw gap, if you have to.
3. With the pre-draw gap established for 17 yards and having shot two or three ends of four arrows at this distance, practice at mixed distances for the rest of the period. For example, shoot two arrows at 17 yards and the other two at 10 yards. On the next end, shoot one arrow at 10 yards, one at 14 yards, one at 15 yards, and one at 17 yards. Keep on shooting at different distances, always using the pre-draw gap system. The instructor should continue to pass up and down the line, encouraging all, correcting mistakes as necessary, and making use of student assistants when good ones are available and can help.

LESSON VII

OBJECT: To learn to make proper adjustments in pre-draw gap for different distances.

1. Warm up with the exercisers, drawing thirty-five to forty times.
2. Start shooting at 20 yards, using the same pre-draw gap used at 17 yards. It will probably work. If not, adjust to one that does. Girls using straight wooden or solid fiber glass bows of 20-lb. pull may find the gap moving up or decreasing—perhaps disappearing.
3. Spend the rest of the class period shooting at mixed distances. Shoot one end at 20 yards, one end at 15 yards, and one end at 10 yards. Try other distances in between and beyond. If class time permits, try one or more four-position "walkups." (Shoot one arrow at 20 yards, one at 17 yards, one at 15 yards, and one at 10 yards.)

   Note: Some archers with very weak bows may now find that on distances of 20 yards and longer their pre-draw gap has decreased, and in some cases may have disappeared altogether, and that at pre-draw, the arrow point is on the target. This is to be expected. Students should make the necessary adjustment and keep the instructor informed.

LESSON VIII

OBJECT: To give opportunity for the instructor to give individual coaching.

The students should practice at the distances for which the class as a whole feels most need. The instructor and assistants should concentrate on coaching individuals who need it.

LESSON IX

OBJECT: To give the first test.

1. Warm up with the exercisers, drawing forty to forty-five times.
2. It is suggested that for the test the Operation Archery Modified Flint Round be used. Note: Table A–1 is an outline of this test.

TABLE A–1

Operation Archery Modified Flint Round Score Card
(total of seven targets at 12- and 18-inch faces, total of twenty-eight arrows) *

Shooting Distance	No. of Arrows	Target Size	Hits	Score	Shooting Station (Sequence)
17 yards	4	18″	_____	_____	1st
20 feet	4	12″	_____	_____	2d
20 yards	4	18″	_____	_____	3d
14 yards	4	12″	_____	_____	4th
15 yards	4	18″	_____	_____	5th
10 yards	4	12″	_____	_____	6th
20, 17, 15 and 10 yards	1 at each distance	18″	======	======	7th
	Total		_____	_____	

* Similar to the N.F.A.A. Modified Flint Round, but with 12- and 18-inch faces (collegiate and scholastic modification) substituted for 6- and 8-inch faces and with minor yardage variation for the four-position walkup target. The larger faces were adopted for teaching field archery in schools and colleges because they result in more hits and good morale.

An explanation of the layout for the test is here presented. Previous to the arrival of students, the archery range should be set up and prepared as follows: Six targets should be on the target line at least 15 feet apart from center to center. Each target should have stapled to it two field archery target faces, one 18 inches in diameter and one 12 inches in diameter. On target #1, the 18-inch face should be stapled above the 12-inch face. On targets #3 and #5, the faces should be stapled on the same way. On targets #2, #4, and #6, however, the 12-inch face should be stapled above the 18-inch face. In other words, on every other target the faces should be reversed.

Six different shooting lines should be set up parallel to the target line and numbered at each end. Shooting line No. 1 (from which the class shoots first and at the 18-inch face) should be 17 yards from the target line. Shooting line No. 2 (from which the class shoots the second and at the 12-inch face) should be 20 feet from the target line. Shooting line No. 3 should be 20 yards from the target line, and from this distance students shoot at the 18-inch face. Next, the class should shoot at the 12-inch face from shooting line No. 4, which is 14 yards from the target line. Then from line No. 5, which is 15 yards from the targets, students shoot at the 18-inch face. From line No. 6, which is 10 yards from the targets, they shoot at the small face, which is 12 inches.

If the instructor has the layout ready as above outlined before the class arrives, the test can be completed in one class period of 35 to 40 minutes.

Take the class through the test, shooting four arrows each from each shooting line or station in the order indicated (1 to 6) and record their scores. After the class has shot the four arrows from line No. 6 at 10 yards, they shoot the four-position "walkup," which differs from the previous ends in that one arrow is shot from line No. 3 (20 yards); one arrow from line or station No. 1, which is from 17 yards; one arrow from station No. 5, which is 15 yards from the targets; and one arrow from station No. 6, which is 10 yards from the targets. All four arrows in the four-position "walkup" are shot at the large 18-inch face. With the shooting and scoring of the "walkup," the test involving the shooting of the Operation Archery Modified Flint Round is over. (Fig. A–15 shows a useful class scorecard.)

LESSON X

OBJECT: To train students to quickly adapt pre-draw gaps to different shooting distances.

1. Warm up with the exercisers, drawing the elbow back forty to forty-five times.
2. Spend the entire period shooting at different distances from 7 to 25 yards, experimenting with the pre-draw gap aiming system for bare-bow shooting without keeping scores.

    Before shooting at any distance, remind the students (as needed) to concentrate on the following and in this sequence:

    a) Adjust the *pre-draw* aim to the proper gap for correct elevation.
    b) Shift attention to center of the target and keep looking there.
    c) Hold the bow at the elevation determined in a above without any change in elevation while the arrow is drawn back to proper anchor.
    d) Establish and maintain the proper tilt (cant) of the bow (too much cant of bow in a right-handed archer tends to shoot the arrow to the right, whereas too little cant may shoot it to the left). Have right-handed students try tilting bow about 20 degrees to the right of vertical.
    e) Execute a consistent live smooth release and a good afterhold. Instructor and assistants should coach students constantly on all seven fundamentals.

LESSON XI

OBJECT: To add interest by shooting from kneeling position at different distances and keeping score.

1. Warm up as usual with the exercisers.

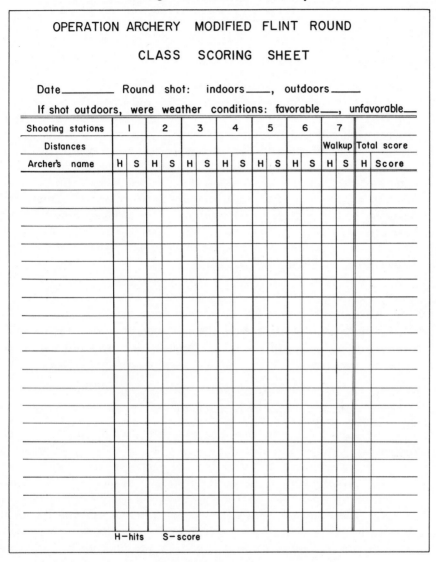

OPERATION ARCHERY MODIFIED FLINT ROUND

CLASS SCORING SHEET

Date_____ Round shot: indoors_____, outdoors_____

If shot outdoors, were weather conditions: favorable___, unfavorable___

Shooting stations	1		2		3		4		5		6		7			
Distances													Walkup		Total score	
Archer's name	H	S	H	S	H	S	H	S	H	S	H	S	H	S	H	Score

H—hits   S—score

Fig. A–15. Field archery class scoring sheet.

2. Have the class shoot four arrows at 10 yards, keeping score. Have the class move back to 15 yards, shoot four arrows, and score. Move back to 25 yards and shoot one arrow; then another at 20 yards, another at 15 yards, and the fourth arrow at 10 yards. Score the hits.

3. Shoot one arrow at a 12-inch face at 10-yards distance. Move back to 15 yards, kneel on the right knee, and shoot two arrows at the 18-inch target face. Move back to 20 yards and shoot the final arrow while standing. Score all the arrows and record their total value in the rollbook.

4. Spend the rest of the class period shooting at varying distances from a kneeling position.

LESSON XII

OBJECT: To establish the pre-draw aiming spot for 25 yards.

1. Warm up as usual with the exercisers.
2. Shoot three ends of four arrows each at 20 yards, using the pre-draw gap.
3. Step back to 25 yards and try the same pre-draw gap at 20 yards. At this distance with college bows, particularly with girls, more students will find that the pre-draw gap will have decreased to almost none; possibly the arrow point will be on the bull's-eye itself. Use the aiming center or middle of the bull's-eye for your pre-draw aiming spot if this is it. The pre-draw aiming spot at 25 yards might still be below the center of the target for archers with good bows; above it for archers whose bows have poor cast.
4. Shoot at 25 yards for the rest of the class period, using whatever is the correct pre-draw aiming elevation.

LESSON XIII

OBJECT: To help each student find the distance at which each can use the aiming center of the target for his pre-draw aiming spot (pre-draw gap zero).

It must be realized that this distance will vary with different students, with different bows, and with different sets of arrows.

1. Start the class shooting at 20 yards, assuming that at this distance each student will need to use a pre-draw gap below the aiming center of the target. Shoot one end at 20 yards, then one end at 21 yards, then an end at 22 yards. Students should inform the instructor as soon as their pre-draw gap starts decreasing. Keep moving away from the target 1 yard at a time, shooting an end of four arrows at each new distance. Eventually, all students will reach a distance at which the pre-draw gap will disappear because the pre-draw aiming spot will be right on the middle of the bull's-eye. This might be called the pre-draw gap zero (0) or the "pre-draw point blank," but it is not to be confused with the *point blank* range of a bow. As each student reaches this point ("pre-draw point blank"), he should notify the instructor. When several students have found this distance and have notified the instructor, he should stop all shooting and explain what is happening. See Figs. 2–9 and 2–10 for illustrations of this condition. As students step back to greater and greater distances than the one at which they experienced the pre-draw point blank, their pre-draw gap will now increase again but will be moving upward *above* the center of the target.
2. Have the class continue shooting for the rest of the period, everyone attempting to find the distance at which their pre-draw elevation is exactly on the middle of the bull's-eye (pre-draw gap zero, or pre-draw point blank).

LESSON XIV

OBJECT: Use of the pre-draw gap system in playing the game "Roving Ball."

Prepare, before the class meets, six balls 4 inches in diameter. Make them by crumpling papers or rags into a round mass and by winding string tightly around them until the diameter of each ball becomes about 4 inches. To finish off the wrapping with the string, thread the last 3-foot length of string onto a big darning needle and poke or sew it through the ball several times in different places and then tie the end of the string to one of the previously sewn stitches.

Divide the class into six teams, giving each team one of the balls. Each participant carries his bow and one arrow. One person on each team carries extra arrows for use in case some are broken or lost.

This game requires lots of field space. Start the six teams out in various directions that are safe for shooting, free from other people and from hazards like rocks that would break arrows. Each person on the four- or five-member team has a shooting order, or turn at kicking the ball out where it can be shot at. Do not try to see how far it can be kicked, at least in the early part of the game. After the ball has been kicked out and stops rolling, each team member shoots an arrow at the ball. Anyone hitting the ball scores 5 point. Of those whose arrows miss the ball, the one coming closest gets 3 points, the person whose arrow comes next closest scores 2 points, the next closest 1 point, and the rest no points.

The next team member takes his turn kicking the ball in a safe direction; and all shoot their one arrow again, keeping score as previously indicated. Continue this game throughout the class period, using the pre-draw gap system of aiming.

LESSON XV

OBJECT: Competition between target groups at different distances.

1. Warm up as usual with the exercisers.
2. Using the pre-draw gap system, make a few practice shots at distances from 7 steps to 20 yards. Keep scores and have competition between target groups or teams if there are the same number of students on each target.

LESSON XVI

OBJECT: Give second test (mid-term).

1. Have range set up for the test before students arrive.
2. Repeat the test as described in Lesson IX.

LESSON XVII

OBJECT: To have each student determine his or her *post-draw gap* at the same distance at which they "pre-draw gap zero" (pre-draw point blank).

1. Warm up as usual with exercisers.
2. Practice shooting one or two ends of four arrows each at the distance each student can use the center of the bull's-eye as his pre-draw aiming spot (pre-draw point blank). In doing this, however, have them shoot in three different groups. Group A: those who can use the center of the bull's-eye as their pre-draw aiming spot or pre-draw gap zero at 20 yards or within a pace up or back from it. Group B:. those who pre-draw gap zero at approximately 23 yards. Group C: those who pre-draw point blank at 25 or 26 yards. With fewer students in these more homogeneous groups, they can spread out farther and be safe even if not shooting from the exact same distances. If safety is in doubt, each of the three groups should shoot separately.
3. Have the students stand at the same distance at which they pre-draw gap zero and take their pre-draw aim at the center of the bull's-eye, and then as usual draw the string and arrow back to the anchor without changing position of the bow arm. *Next,* still without moving anything or shooting, look down over the pile of the now fully drawn (post-drawn) arrow and observe the width of the vertical gap between the point of the arrow and the target face. This apparent vertical distance from the pile of the arrow to the target is the post-draw gap. It might be one, two, or three target diameters.

The instructor should explain to the students that as they gradually move back farther and farther from this distance and shoot, the post-draw gap will become progressively narrower until it eventually disappears altogether. The distance at which the post-draw gap reaches zero and at which an archer can use the center of the bull's-eye for his post-draw aiming spot is the *"post-draw point blank"* or *true point blank,* as usually referred to in archery. This again will vary with different archers, different bows, and different sets of arrows.

The instructor should explain the relationships that exist between the pre-draw gap; the "pre-draw point blank"; the post-draw gap; and the "post-draw point blank," true point blank. The archer should strive through experimental practice to discover the distances at which the above relationships exist with his school bow (and with his own hunting bow if he has one). He should now realize and understand why the class was started using the pre-draw gap system, and its superiority over the post-draw gap system for use at the shorter distances (good for hunting), and why the post-draw gap is best for the longer distances. Having practiced shooting at various distances using pre- and post-draw gaps, and having established and experimented and practiced at the distances at which one can use "pre-draw point blank" and "post-draw point blank," one should practice shooting instinctively. One should concentrate the eyes on the spot to be hit, draw back (executing each of the seven fundamentals in sequence), and shoot without being conscious of the steps taken in shooting—either the pre- or the post-draw gap system. It will be surprising how well and accurately the individual will shoot instinctively with practice. If the archer finds his shooting inconsistent, he should practice more with the pre- and post-draw gaps to further educate his bow hand and carefully check his seven fundamentals in sequence.

LESSON XVIII

OBJECT: To add interest and variety by having competition in shooting balloons.

Before class starts have class members inflate about fifty or sixty round balloons to a diameter of about 6 or 7 inches and fasten six balloons to each target butt with a very short string.

Start the class shooting at 20 yards. Have each archer shoot two ends of four arrows each at 20 yards, 15 yards, and 10 yards respectively. Determine which group of archers first breaks all the balloons on their target, or which group of archers breaks the largest number of balloons in the completed round of twenty-four arrows shot. In the latter case, the instructor must replenish balloons broken after each end, so that at the start of each end of four arrows, there are always six inflated balloons at which to shoot.

LESSON XIX

OBJECT: To play "Buddy Tic-Tac-Toe."

Staple to each of six targets a large piece of wrapping paper 24 to 36 inches in diameter on which has been painted, with black poster paint (tempera works well) or with ink felt-point pen, two parallel lines 10 inches apart crossed in the middle with two other parallel lines 10 inches apart perpendicular to the first parallel lines (#). Each archer should have six arrows for this game. Assuming that there are four archers on each target, have two buddies on one target team up against the other two buddies on the same target. From a distance of 10 yards, the two pairs of buddies on each target compete in "Tic-Tac-Toe" (three in a row). Archer No. 1 of the "A" buddies shoots one arrow, then archer No. 1 of "B" buddies shoots an arrow, then archer No. 2 of "A" buddies shoots followed by archer No. 2 of "B" buddies.

Using this same shooting order (alternating teams of archers 1, 3, 2, and 4), continue shooting until one pair of buddies, "A" or "B," first gets three of their arrows in a row in the "Tic-Tac-Toe" double cross, or until all of the six arrows of each archer have been shot. The same teams of buddies should compete over again, and probably a third time, to become thoroughly familiar with the game. After the third game has been completed with competition only between buddies on the same target, winners on all the targets can compete with the winning buddies on other targets, and losing buddies against losing buddies on other targets.

In this game as in all other archery games, extreme care must be taken relative to all safety measures. No archer should advance in front of the shooting line at any time to check his scores on the target until all archers have shot all of their arrows and the instructor blows the whistle to retrieve arrows. In like manner, no arrows should be shot in starting the game until the instructor gives the signal. A double blast of the whistle is a signal for all shooting to stop immediately. It is used as an emergency signal.

LESSON XX

OBJECT: To practice for the final test, and give instructor an opportunity to check students' shooting form.

Practice shooting the Operation Archery Modified Flint Round, since it will again be used as the third and final practical or shooting test for the course in field archery. Instructors should, as need arises, check their students on their shooting form. Keep score and have informal competition between the different target teams to add enjoyment to the shooting.

LESSON XXI

OBJECT: To introduce the "Roving Deer" game, requiring use of bare-bow technique—a game of fun.

Play in teams of four to six students. Have one "deer" to each team. The deer consists of a potato sack or bag stuffed three-fourths full of dry leaves or straw with the open end tightly tied shut with one end of a 6-foot length of ¼-inch rope so that 2 to 3 feet are left hanging at the other end from the knot end as a tail. Three 4-inch diameter spots should be painted in black on the bag as its middle, and each of the spots should be equidistant from each other. This is so that there will always be one spot facing the shooter, regardless of how the deer lies. Permission should be secured from a farmer to use his mowed field or meadow if the athletic field is too small or crowded for safe conduct of the game. Teams play as isolated units, starting far enough apart to be safely out of each other's way. Each team appoints a scorer (who keeps record of each team member's score) and a captain who officiates and decides whether or not it is safe to shoot at the deer in the spot it lies (whether there are rocks under it or near it that would break arrows, or whether or not it lies a safe distance from some other team).

A shooting order is established (including the captain), and each player takes his turn at grasping the "deer" by the tail (rope), swinging it around one or more times to gather momentum, and throwing it as far or as near as he wishes. All players nock one arrow and each tries to hit the "deer" in the heart (black spot), shooting from behind the place from which it was thrown. Each hit in the heart scores 5 points, and any other hits on the bag score 3 points. If the player whose turn it was to throw the deer cannot throw the deer as far as desired, he or she may ask team members to walk back an additional number of steps to increase the distance to the deer; and the players must comply with this request. Compare scores to determine the winners in each group as well as the winning team.

LESSON XXII

OBJECT: To try bare-bow or instinctive shooting at various distances without conscious use of pre- or post-draw gap.

Have students practice at short ranges (7 steps, 10 yards, 14 yards, 15 yards, 17 yards, and 20 yards), using the purely instinctive system, and check their execution of the seven fundamentals. Mix the distances; move from one distance to another in the most unexpected ways. Shoot several ends from the kneeling position (down on right knee if right-handed). Shoot all distances 10 yards or less at the 12-inch target faces, and all distances over 10 yards at the 18-inch faces.

LESSON XXIII

OBJECT: Practice before final test.

Use the class-time practicing by shooting at some of the distances to be used in the third and final test as were used in the ninth and sixteenth lessons. Review the seven fundamentals, having them demonstrated by different students in the class.

Have the students do some more shooting at various distances, checking up on their form on the fundamentals. This will be their last class-time opportunity for such coaching.

LESSON XXIV

Give the third and final test as set up in the ninth and sixteenth lessons. Shoot a regulation Operation Archery Round to determine the class champions.

LESSON XXV

Give final written examination on rules, techniques, safety procedures, etc.

Note: In case of rain on the day of Lesson XXIV, the day for which the final practical test was planned, give the written examination on the rainy day and finish up with the practical shooting test on the last day of the class.

MISCELLANEOUS SUGGESTIONS

In case you have a regulation Field Archery Round course on the campus or within 10 miles of the campus, substitute fourteen or twenty-eight targets of this for lessons involving either "Roving Ball," "Buddy Tic-Tac-Toe," or "Shooting Balloons," as it will be more rewarding. The local Field Archery Club will invite your class to come out and observe their tournaments or better yet to participate in them.

If the Field Roving Course is a long way from the campus, it will be necessary to arrange a special trip for this experience, starting in the afternoon on a weekday, or on a week end, and having a cook-out meal or picnic with a campfire following the event. Other games, some of which may be substituted for games listed in these lessons, will be found at the end of Chapter 3.

RAINY DAY PROGRAMS

Many items can be taught indoors on rainy days, such as: knots archers should know and use; how to make bowstrings; how to repair fletchings on arrows; how to replace piles; how to measure bow weights (perhaps have class help measure all bow weights and marks them on tape on bows); how to serve strings; how to put a knot above nocking point; make and discuss charts or blackboard drawings showing relationships of pre-draw gap and post-draw gap at short and long distances; hold a form clinic and review fine points of form in shooting.

First National Field Archery Champions

The First National Championship Tournament of the N.F.A.A. was held at Allegan, Michigan, August 10 to 12, 1946 (Fig. B–1). It was the biggest archery event in modern history, with 476 registrants. This tournament literally exploded field archery into the sporting world. Those who already were in field archery knew its possibilities, but the public had not previously realized the lure of the sport that within a few short years was to become the nation's fastest growing sport. Leading target groups literally were swamped by the large gallery of enthusiastic spectators.

Fig. B–1. Windshield stickers as above were displayed by those who competed in the First National Tournament. (Sketch courtesy of Michigan Department of Conservation.)

When the grueling 3-day meet was all over, the First National Field Archery Champions were:

Men: Dr. Erwin Pletcher, Bakersfield, California. Score—2183
Women: Mrs. "Babe" Bitzenburger, Los Angeles, California. Score—1152

Jr. Boy: Maurice LeFavor, Ft. Wayne, Indiana. Score—1199
Jr. Girl: Kathleen Powell, Portland, Oregon. Score—428

Archery tackle used at the tournament seems of historic interest. Hunting-weight equipment predominated. Sixty per cent of the men's bows were over 50 lbs. in pull; 96 per cent over 45 lbs. Only four men's bows were lighter than 40 lbs. Most women were shooting bows with draw weights between 30 and 45 lbs. Everything considered, the First National was a tournament of bare-bow archers. Scores were nothing to brag about by present-day standards, but all those who competed in the tournament had a whale of a time.

Fig. B–2. First and three-time N.F.A.A. champion field archer Erwin Pletcher of California. Here he demonstrates his instinctive form of archery. (Photograph by W. Leon Riegler.)

Fig. B–3. First and four-time National champion field archer "Babe" Bitzenberger of California demonstrates her instinctive shooting form. (Photograph by W. Leon Riegler.)

Fig. B–4. The First National Field Archery Championship Tournament ended with these three Californians on top. They are (*left to right*) Roy Hoff, 3d place winner and editor of *Archery* magazine; Erwin Pletcher, the Champion; and Ken Moore, 2d place winner and former Mail Tournament Champion. (Photograph by W. Leon Riegler.)

Fig. B–5. George Marks and tournament chairman Karl Palmatier, both of Michigan, here discuss scoring problems at the First National. (Photograph by W. Leon Riegler.)

Fig. B–6. N.F.A.A. officials at the First National included (*left to right*) A. J. Michelson, Flint, Michigan, president; Arnold O. Haugen, Lansing, Michigan, Midwest regional representative; John Yount, Redlands, California, secretary-treasurer; and W. B. Wescott, Dover, Massachusetts, vice-president. (Photograph by W. Leon Riegler.)

APPENDIX C

Necedah Archery Shoots

The Necedah Shoot, a festive-type archery tournament with bowhunting tackle, has become a firmly established annual event in Wisconsin. Its popularity has spread until it is now shot at special bowhunters' meetings in several states. Wisconsin's "Bow Hunters" are the proud sponsors of the Necedah event in that state, but in the beginning it was the brainchild of Roy Case, historically prominent archer of Racine, Wisconsin.

When the shoot first was held in 1946, even though only a week's notice was provided, 151 archers showed up to join in the fun. Howard Trapp, then president of the Wisconsin "Bow Hunters," and Roy Case had hurriedly prepared the course of 16 targets, using a bulldozer to heap up mounds of dirt for backstops. Little did they realize as they toiled that history was in the making.

The idea behind the shoot was to give bowhunters a chance to try out their hunting tackle a few days prior to each deer season and to shoot at life-sized cardboard deer in realistic surroundings. Each participant was required to use his or her regular hunting tackle. A maximum of two arrows at each target was permitted, but the second was not shot if the first scored. Values were highest for the first arrow, yielding 10 points for a hit in a circle on the heart and lung area, 4 for other parts of the body cavity, and 2 for hits in the remaining parts. Values were reduced to half these scores if the hit were made with the second arrow.

When the Second Annual Necedah Shoot was held in 1947, 455 archers swamped the affair. Popularity has continued with the festive atmosphere growing year by year, attracting archers from distant states. It is not certain whether it is the shoot or the carnival-like atmosphere that has contributed most to success. Wisconsin bowhunters, however, have shown that they will turn out en masse, whether it's for their annual convention (without shooting) or for their special Necedah Shoot. Wisconsin's hunters indeed are fun loving.

Badger State archers have shown that bowhunters if given an opportunity will come from great distances to attend a shoot where joviality and friendship are the principal rewards. Winning the shoot apparently is not the main attraction. It is to be hoped that more bowmen will allow archery to produce the real enjoyment and fellowship it has to offer. There is no need

for the sober tension and "dog eat dog" atmosphere that so commonly pre-
vails at championship tournaments.

The principal value of the Necedah Shoot is probably as a novelty
tournament for an annual bowhunters get-together. To shoot it more
often might ruin its attractiveness.

APPENDIX D

Sportsmanship in Archery

THE LANDOWNERS GUARANTEE

Means for providing the best of relations between bowhunters and landowners were provided in 1951. The N.F.A.A. Executive Committee established the "Landowner's Guarantee Against Property Damage," a guarantee to farmer-landowners that each and every member of the Association will conduct himself as a gentleman and a sportsman. The need for such a forward step by sportsmen's organizations had been felt by many, but history of bad conduct by a few outlaws had made a good conduct guarantee by any national association seem a bad risk.

The N.F.A.A., however, had confidence that the quality of sportsmanship of its general membership was such that a guarantee could safely be provided. Accordingly, the guarantee was adopted and printed on each membership card. It reads as follows:

LANDOWNERS GUARANTEE AGAINST PROPERTY DAMAGE

The National Field Archery Association has confidence that our member, whose name appears on the front of this card, is a gentleman and a sportsman. May we request that you allow him to hunt with bow and arrow on your property, with the understanding that if he in any way damages your property or livestock, and refuses to make settlement, we will, upon presentation of his name and proof of damages, pay for said damages up to the amount of $100.00.

Good only for life of membership.

The membership card continues with instructions to the member as follows:

It should be understood that the guarantee on the reverse of this card is not an insurance policy. It is, when presented to a landowner, a promise to conduct yourself as a sportsman should, backed up by your fellow archers, who have faith in your good sportsmanship. We don't believe we have a member who thinks so little of the friendship of his fellow members as to violate this faith.

This gesture of presenting one's membership card with a guarantee and implied good conduct, whenever requesting permission to hunt, was a move in the right direction to create friendly relations between farmers and bowhunters.

It is now apparent that the confidence that the N.F.A.A. had in its members was well justified, because after 10 years of operation of the guarantee, not a single claim has been made against the association. This is even better than had been hoped for.

A high degree of sportsmanship by both members of the N.F.A.A. and non-members has been exhibited by bowhunters across the nation. A couple of examples will suffice: In the first 8 years of bowhunting in Michigan, not a single arrest and prosecution for game law violation occurred. Iowa bowhunters similarly carried a record clear of convictions during the first 6 seasons.

HAMPERING RESTRICTIONS HAVE THORNS

It is unfortunate that many violations charged against bowhunters are really violations involving what may be regarded as hampering restrictions. Such restrictions have little if any foundation or need so far as good conservation principles and practices are concerned. The requirement in a couple of states that hunting bows must be unstrung and/or in a case when transported in a car falls under this category. There is no measure of safety involved, and these restrictions have no value or need so far as saving deer is concerned.

Violations of even these restrictions, however, bring on adverse public opinion. To keep our records of conduct good and above reproach, we must obey all restrictions. It is up to archers themselves to help police their ranks and keep violations to a minimum.

Hampering restrictions were brought about by a few unscrupulous individuals who "road hunted" deer at night. Then too, the existence of such restrictions may be partly the result of uninformed individuals who insisted that since guns had to be unloaded and in a case, bows should be treated likewise. Such reasoning to justify the restrictions is fallacious. The unloading and casing of guns concern public safety in cars and on the highways and is meant to prevent shooting deer from cars. This has conservation values.

So long as hampering restrictions are in effect, they must be obeyed to the letter of the law. If there are laws that do not make sense or that seem unjust, we should combine forces to get them repealed through improved legislation. If and when improved regulations are needed, they are worth fighting for.

GOOD SPORTSMANSHIP AWARD

One of the biggest jobs in any organization is to improve sportsmanship. Recognition of fair play and good sportsmanship is a most desirable activity. The N.F.A.A. has provided leadership in promoting and recognizing outstanding sportsmanship. By adopting the Rules of Fair Chase as a model for hunting, a sense of fair play has been encouraged.

Individuals with outstanding records for good sportsmanship have been singled out for recognition with special awards—the Good Sportsmanship Medal. To date three individuals most deserving of such honors have been given recognition. They are:

Edwin "Nubbie" Pate, California, 1947 (Fig. D–1)
Ed. Dries, Texas, 1948
Guy McMinemy, Illinois, 1953

Fig. D–1. The first Good Sportsmanship Medal of the N.F.A.A. was awarded Edwin "Nubbie" Pate *(left)* of Barstow, California, at the Second National Tournament, 1947. Presenting the award is the late W. B. Wescott, vice-president of the N.F.A.A. (Photograph by W. Leon Riegler.)

COMPTON MEDAL OF HONOR

The Compton Medal of Honor was established by the N.F.A.A. in 1947 as the most highly esteemed award in all archery. It was decreed that, "It shall be bestowed sparingly and only in recognition of outstanding and unselfish contributions to archery in any of its phases."

In naming the Compton Medal of Honor, the N.F.A.A. paid special and lasting tribute to W. J. "Chief" Compton, recognizing him as a patron saint to field and hunting archery (Fig. D–2). It was Compton who taught such archery greats as Dr. Saxton Pope, Art Young, and Stanley Spencer.

Fig. D–2.   The Compton Medal of Honor awarded for outstanding services to archery.   (Photograph by Floyd Thomas.)

To date eleven N.F.A.A. members have been singled out for Compton Medal Awards.   Recipients are the following:

George Brommers, Washington, 1947
Roy Case, Wisconsin, 1948
A. J. Michelson, Michigan, 1949
W. B. Wescott, Massachusetts, 1952
Karl Palmatier, Michigan, 1952
Tracey Stalker, Michigan, 1953
John Yount, California, 1955
Glenn St. Charles, Washington, 1958
Dr. A. O. Haugen, Iowa, 1959
Roy Hoff, California, 1962
Dr. Paul Klopsteg, Illinois, 1962

Glossary

ANCHOR, n.—The place on the face to which the hand drawing the string and arrow is fitted at full draw preparatory to aiming and releasing.

ANCHOR, v.—To fix the hand at the drawing point.

ARMGUARD—A piece of stiff material worn at the inner side of the wrist of the bow arm to protect the wrist from becoming bruised by the string.

ARROWHEAD—The striking end of an arrow, usually a separate part fastened to the shaft.

ARROW-CREST—The identifying mark or marks near the vanes of an arrow, usually a combination of colored rings.

BACK (bow)—The side of the bow away from the string.

BARE-BOW DIVISION—A group of archers competing with bows devoid of any mark or sighting device for aid in shooting.

BELLY (bow)—The side of the bow facing the string.

BIRD SHOT—A field archery target with 6-inch faces and shot with one arrow from each of 20, 25, 30, and 35 feet.

BLUNT POINT—A flat-tipped arrow point with parallel sides and without cutting edges.

BOW HAND OR ARM—The hand or arm that holds the bow in shooting.

BOWHUNTER—One who hunts with bow and arrow.

BOWSTRING—A cord (usually of fortisan thread) fastened between the nocks at the ends of a bow to force it into a bent and stressed condition. Its use is for drawing the bow and driving the arrow forward when released.

BRACE (bow), v.—To make a bow ready for shooting by bending its limbs so as to permit proper attaching of the bowstring.

BRACER—*See* ARMGUARD.

BROADHEAD—A pointed and sharp-edged arrowhead with its edges diverging toward its base. It is used primarily for hunting predators, big game, and game birds.

BUTT—The backstop to which a target face is fastened, consisting of straw or excelsior bales, a target matt, sod, or a dirt bank.

COURSE, n.—An aggregate of fourteen field archery targets or some multiple of that number; the series of targets serving for field archery practice or competition.

CREEP, v.—To permit an arrow to move forward from full draw, thereby losing some of the effective length of draw and tension while aiming and prior to releasing the arrow.

DEAD RELEASE—A release of the bowstring in which the drawing hand remains locked immovably on the anchor point.

ELEVATION—The inclination of a drawn arrow in its vertical plane.

FACE—Short for target face.

FEATHERING—The vanes on an arrow. Most commonly of turkey primary feathers but sometimes of plastic material.

FIBERGLASS—A material made up of fine strands of glass bound together by a gluelike matrix. Commonly used as a surface lamination or for the entire material in bow construction.

FIELD ARCHER—A person who shoots on field archery courses or who shoots at random marks as he roves through fields and forests.

FIELD ARROW—An arrow with parallel or spike-tipped point that is used for field or roving archery. Usually more rugged than target-type arrows.

FIELD CAPTAIN—The official in charge of a field archery tournament. He is the final authority in directing the tournament and in interpreting rules and regulations of the N.F.A.A.

FINGERTAB—*See* TAB.

FISTMELE—The breadth of the fist with the thumb extended, usually measuring about 6 or 7 inches. Used to indicate the height to which a bow should be strung. The distance between the bow handle and the string.

FLETCHING—*See* FEATHERING.

FOUR-POSITION (shot)—A target at which each of the four arrows are shot from a different stake; or, if shot from one stake, they are each shot at a different butt.

FREEZING—The assumption of immobility at the last instant of aiming, resulting in inability to complete proper aiming.

GAP—The vertical space an archer sees between the tip of his arrow and the target.

GAP, POST-DRAW—The vertical distance or gap an archer sees between the tip of his aimed arrow and the target to be hit when viewed with the arrow fully drawn and at anchor.

GAP, PRE-DRAW—The vertical distance or gap seen between the tip of the undrawn arrow and the mark to be hit when observed with the arrow nocked, the bow arm extended toward the target, the drawing fingers contacting the string, and the bow arm elevated properly for a hit.

GLANCE-INS—An arrow ricocheting into the target after hitting some object in its line of flight. Not allowed any scoring value.

GLOVE (shooting)—An archer's glove for protecting the fingers drawing the bowstring. Usually consists of three leather fingers attached to a wrist strap.

GRIP—The manner in which the bow hand contacts the bow, or the manner of grasping the bow as hard grip or loose grip.

HEAVY TACKLE DIVISION—A competitive division for archers using arrows of a weight suitable for hunting, the actual weight depending on arrow length. No aiming device is permitted. Arrows 28 inches in length must weigh 1 ounce.

HOLD, n.—A pause at full draw to permit aiming before loosing.

HOLD, v.—To pause for aiming.

HUNTING ARROW—An arrow designed for hunting: blunt-tipped for small game and with broadheads for ducks, pheasants, predators, and big game.

HUNTING BOW—A bow of such strength as to be suitable for hunting; often shorter than target and field bows so as to be easily handled and shot in brush. Some states require a minimum draw weight.

INTERMEDIATE ARCHER—In field archery, an archer of 15 through 17 years of age.

JUNIOR ARCHER—An archer 12 through 14 years.

LIVE RELEASE—A loose or release of the bowstring in which the drawing hand recoils or moves backward along the cheek about 2 or more inches but stays in contact with the face.

MEDITERRANEAN DRAW—The draw in which the index, long, and ring fingers are used to grasp and pull the bowstring, with the arrow nock resting between the first and second fingers.

NOCK, n.—(1) The notches at the ends of a bow into which the bowstring ends fit. (2) The slot in the rear end of an arrow into which the bowstring fits. (3) The notches, ferule or plastic, or metal to be attached to the feathered end of an arrow.

Nock, v.—(1) The slipping of the bowstring loop into the notch at the tip of the bow when stringing. (2) To fit an arrow to the bowstring.

Overbowed—The condition of shooting a bow that is too strong for the archer, resulting in straining, poor postural stance, inconsistent and inaccurate shooting.

Overdraw—To draw an arrow back on the bow until its tip slips off and behind the arrow-rest. A dangerous condition, which may break the arrow and result in injury to the bow hand, arm, or face.

Overshoot—To shoot over and beyond the mark.

Pass-Through—An arrow that penetrates a target to the extent that its scoring position on the target face no longer can be seen.

Peeking—The jerking of the head from its position at release in order to watch where the arrow hits. A bad habit.

Pile—A socketed arrowhead without cutting edges, usually cylindrical or conoidal and either pointed or blunt.

Pluck (release)—A jerking release or loose of the bowstring with the drawing hand often moving sideways and away from the anchor.

Point Blank—The distance at which an archer aims the tip of his arrow, at full draw, directly on the mark to be hit.

Pre-Draw Aiming Spot—The spot or elevation to which a nocked arrow is held preparatory to drawing the bow in pre-draw gap style of bowshooting.

Quiver—A receptacle to hold arrows conveniently for shooting. A back quiver is hung on the back, a side quiver is fastened at the belt, a pocket quiver fits into the hip pocket, and a bow quiver is fastened to the bow. A ground quiver rests on the ground and a floor quiver on the floor.

Rabbit Shot—The field target with 6-inch faces and shot at from distances of 20, 25, 30, and 35 feet. Also called bird shot.

Range—(1) A place for shooting archery. (2) The distance of the mark from the archer.

Rebound—An arrow that bounces off the target without piercing and remaining in the target.

Relaxed Grip—The hold on the bow in which the handle of the bow rests on the inner edge of the pad of the thumb, with contact through the base of the palm between the two pads of flesh. The thumb and index fingers encircle the bow handle to control the bow, yet give it freedom of action.

Round (field)—Twenty-eight targets of shooting, consisting of two 14-target units or twice around one 14-target unit. Consists of a total of 112 arrows.

Roving—The art and practice of one who shoots at casual marks at unknown distances such as stumps, weeds, dirt mounds, etc.

Shaft—An arrow.

Shooting Glove—See Glove.

Shooting Line—The line or position from behind which field archers shoot.

Shot—(1) A complete act of shooting. (2) The distance an arrow is cast—as, a 60-yard shot.

Sight Division—The group or aggregate of field archers using a visible sighting device for aiming when shooting. Also called the freestyle division.

Skip-ins—Arrows that ricochet into the target after first hitting the ground. They are not scored.

Smooth Release—A release of an arrow in which the drawing hand automatically recoils backward 3 or more inches, and with the hand gently brushing and remaining in contact with the face. The backward recoil is an automatic reaction as a result of the back muscles continuing to pull until the arrow has left the string. Only the fingertips yield their tension at the instant of the release. Same as live release.

SPINE—A quality in arrows involving a combination of degree of stiffness and springiness.

SPOT—The usual dark aiming spot in the center of field archery targets.

STAKE—The shooting position marker behind which a field archer stands when shooting at the target.

STRING, v.—*See* BRACE.

STRING HAND—The hand that draws the bowstring.

TAB—A flat piece of leather to protect the three string-pulling fingers and it is slotted for the arrow nock. It may have one or two finger holes for holding it in place.

TACKLE—The complete equipment of an archer.

TARGET—A mark or face: a target of straw bales, a round target matt, or a dirt bank for holding a target face.

TASSEL—A 2- to 3-inch bundle of 2- to 4-inch-length pieces of wool yarn attached as a pendant from an archer's belt or quiver and used to wipe dirt from arrows.

TIMBER—Warning call to let other archers know that an arrow is about to be shot at the target next in order.

TRAJECTORY—A path of flight of an arrow.

TWENTY-PIN—An N.F.A.A. award presented to archers shooting all four arrows into the 5-ring of any official target at a distance of 35 or more yards. For the award, the archer must be an N.F.A.A. member and the shoot must be registered.

UNIT—A 14-target course, including all official shots.

UNSTRING—To remove the bowstring from the nock of a bow, permitting it to return to its position of no tension.

WEIGHT (of bow)—The pounds of effort necessary to pull the bowstring back to a distance equal to the length of the arrow an archer effectively draws. Unless marked otherwise, most bows are marked with the pounds of pull indicated for 28 inches of draw.

Index